"*Bread for the Resistance* is a must-read for all Christians committed to bringing about biblically centered justice in the world. These devotionals are powerful readings that help connect our individual faith journeys with our call to transform systems of injustice in the world. In doing so, this book demonstrates the fullness of biblical witness that speaks both to individuals and systems. Donna Barber has provided us an invaluable resource that can be used by church groups, organizers, or individuals for biblically grounding our work for justice as well as expanding our understanding of what biblical justice is. *Bread for the Resistance* also addresses the personal cost in striving for justice by providing a healing balm and nourishment for the soul when we face barriers, burnout, or discouragement. Read, and you will be refreshed!"

Andrea Smith, Evangelicals 4 Justice and NAIITS: An Indigenous Learning Community

"As a Christian leader with a lifelong commitment to whole-gospel discipleship, I often struggle to find a devotional guide that speaks into all aspects of my faith and life. Donna Barber's book is a treasure. Her courageous honesty and vulnerability, rooted in a profound and vibrant relationship with Jesus that leads her into a life of radical faithfulness, brings me home every time. I heartily recommend this book to anyone who needs bread for the journey."

Alexia Salvatierra, coauthor of *Faith-Rooted Organizing*

"Some people write with beautiful words, and others speak through their character. Donna Barber excels at both. She writes with clarity and an unmatched depth of insight and has the reputation and longevity of someone who has something to teach us all. This devotional was exactly what I needed. *Bread for the Resistance* will refresh your soul and become the one book this year you give to everyone you know."

Ken Wytsma, author of *The Myth of Equality*, founder of The Justice Conference

"Donna has experience in sustainable life-giving transformational ministry. Her book has given us the gift of those practices that continue to fuel this work of shalom and justice. Her wisdom is seen in how she invites us to change the world through rebirth, good news, and love while paying attention to the reality of suffering. Donna envisioned and created the devotional that I wish I was given in my toughest days of pastoral and community work."

Sandra Maria Van Opstal, executive director, Chasing Justice

"Donna Barber has written one of the most timely devotionals of our generation. *Bread for the Resistance* will help you stay connected to the sustaining power of God's word so that your prophetic work is always rooted in the grace of God. I guarantee you've never read a devotional like this, and you will come to it over and over again."

Jonathan Brooks, pastor and author of *Church Forsaken*

"In a world of feel-good soundbites and curated social media lives, Donna Barber offers us words that acknowledge the hard work of justice and hope even when change doesn't seem obvious. She can do this because she does the work of justice, walking in faith, and I am so grateful for such a wise guide."

Kathy Khang, author of *Raise Your Voice*

BREAD
FOR THE
RESISTANCE

40 DEVOTIONS FOR JUSTICE PEOPLE

DONNA BARBER

ivp

An imprint of InterVarsity Press
Downers Grove, Illinois

InterVarsity Press
P.O. Box 1400, Downers Grove, IL 60515-1426
ivpress.com
email@ivpress.com

InterVarsity Press® is the book-publishing division of InterVarsity Christian Fellowship/USA®, a movement of students and faculty active on campus at hundreds of universities, colleges, and schools of nursing in the United States of America, and a member movement of the International Fellowship of Evangelical Students. For information about local and regional activities, visit intervarsity.org.

Scriptures marked NKJV are taken from the NEW KING JAMES VERSION (NKJV). Copyright© 1982 by Thomas Nelson, Inc. Used by permission. All rights reserved.

While any stories in this book are true, some names and identifying information may have been changed to protect the privacy of individuals.

Cover design and image composite: David Fassett
Interior design: Daniel van Loon
Images: old wall: © 123foto / E+ / Getty Images
industrial silos: © rrenis2000 / iStock / Getty Images Plus
abstract painted background: © Don Farrall / Digital Vision / Getty Images
woman holding up fist: © PeopleImages / E+ / Getty Images
graphic skyscrapers illustration: © Jutta Kuss / Getty Images

Figure 1 courtesy of Interaction Institute for Social Change (interactioninstitute.org), artist: Angus Maguire (madewithangus.com)

ISBN 978-0-8308-4396-1 (print)
ISBN 978-0-8308-6380-8 (digital)

Printed in the United States of America ∞

Library of Congress Cataloging-in-Publication Data
A catalog record for this book is available from the Library of Congress.

P	19	18	17	16	15	14	13	12	11	10	9	8	7	6	5	4	3	2
Y	35	34	33	32	31	30	29	28	27	26	25	24	23	22	21	20		

This book is dedicated:

To the powerful men and women of God who taught and challenged me through his Word and lived out its teachings before me: Pastor Hiawatha Coleman, Reverend Gregory Johnson, and Thornton and Frances Anderson.

To the mighty women of prayer who instilled in me the discipline of devotion, the necessity of solitude, and the power of the Spirit: Denise Van Dorn and Rachel Barber.

To my comrades in this fight for justice: Lisa Sharon Harper, David and Joy Bailey, Rudy and Juanita Rasmus, and Ken and Tamara Wytsma.

To my bestie, Jen Casselberry, whose loving, persistent "nagging" demanded this idea become a reality.

To my amazing children who fill my life with joy and keep me on my knees: Jessica, Joshua, Joel, Lea, Asha Joy, and Jonathan.

And to my husband and friend, Leroy Barber, whose fire and faith inspire me to believe that not only is it possible to change the world but also that we are required and accountable, as Jesus followers, to do so.

CONTENTS

Introduction: The Bread of Resistance | 1

> # WORSHIP IS PRAYER THAT IS SUNG, CRIED, OR SHOUTED TO THE LORD.

"FALL DOWN"

Scan the QR codes throughout the book and let the music of the powerful worship band Urban Doxology minister to your soul.

THE BREAD OF RESISTANCE

THE MEAT OF SERVICE

Sometimes you get tired. In the midst of the marching and the posting and the blogging and the meetings—yes, the many, many meetings—you get tired. Tired of having to explain it again to people who don't get it. Tired of figuring out the wording and the right tone of voice. Tired of swallowing the frustration that rises like bile in the back of your throat and tired of pushing down the anger or the sorrow or the fear. Sometimes you get tired while pursuing this thing called *justice*, and you just have to pause, breathe, and steal away until the dust kicked up in that day's battle settles. Sometimes you have to take a moment to feed your soul.

I was able to get by with snacking on Sunday morning sermons and sporadic, repetitious prayer when I was schlepping through the dull routines of life—work, eat, sleep, school, eat, sleep, play, eat, sleep. But when I dared to pursue the narrow way of the kingdom, to discover and fulfill purpose, to hear and heed the call, I slowly realized that my spirit required something more substantive and nourishing.

"Doing justice" is often intense and progress painfully slow. For it requires both strength and endurance to accept the mistake, the misquote, and the misunderstanding, or to push through the pain of disappointment . . . again. You must be willing to be a friend without making friends and to find glory in your weakness. Days are sometimes wrought with emotional cuts and bruises, and relationships are often strained or lost. Patience is tested. Courage is tried. Yet love must remain both method and goal.

On those days (every day), this book is meant to be more than a devotional. It's a reminder of the *why* and a suggestion of the *how* for our spiritual disciplines. It's a tool for creating a quiet space, a connection point between our divine contact and our human context. It's an expression of gratitude for the good days and a word of encouragement for the bad, a pat on the back and a kick in the butt. At the very least it's meant to provide the thought, word, and hope that is needed on any given day to keep you on the path, in the game, and going about the work of the high calling of God that is in Christ Jesus.

Jesus said, "I am the bread of life. He who comes to Me shall never hunger, and he who believes in Me shall never thirst" (John 6:35), and "My food is to do the will of Him who sent Me, and to finish His work" (John 4:34). We are fed and strengthened by the Bread of Life to go and do the good works that nourish our souls. Daily work fueled by daily devotion is the meat and bread designed to sustain us through this life.

As you begin or end each day, read and reread each day's Scripture passage (occasionally, you will find verses quoted in my translation, noted as "DT"). Pause and think on the accompanying reflection. Hum the tunes you hear when you scan the QR codes that are sprinkled throughout the book. Taste and chew. Pray and listen to the Spirit, then make note of what you have heard in your notebook or journal. But know that you can't receive the full benefit of the meal until you have digested it by acting on that word in your everyday life.

Eat and may your soul be refreshed, your heart cleansed, your mind renewed, and your courage restored. May you be moved again and again to *do* justice as you respond first to God and then to the needs of others.

PART 1

UNDERSTANDING OUR PURPOSE

"THE EARTH SHALL KNOW"

SUNG BY URBAN DOXOLOGY

1

DEFIANCE

Who will rise up for me against the evildoers?
Who will stand up for me against the workers of iniquity?

Psalm 94:16

READING: PSALM 94:12-23

In 2008, the war film *Defiance* was released by director Edward Zwick. The film is based on the true story of four Belarusian Jewish brothers who manage to escape Nazi forces sweeping through Eastern Europe by taking refuge in a forest. The brothers turn their struggle for survival into a battle against the Nazis. They are joined by an ever-growing crowd of other survivors who, emboldened by the band of brothers, choose to risk their lives to defy the Nazi forces in a fight for freedom.

I was first intrigued and then inspired by this daring and bold resistance to authority. I saw a nobility in their cause—a righteous indignation that moved me. The brothers and their friends were a ragtag bunch who, much like David facing Goliath, appeared to be inadequately armed and poorly matched against the vast and powerful Nazi army. But they were no longer choosing to hide with hopes only of surviving. No, they were choosing to fight so that they might *live*.

I think about the bands of brothers and sisters that rise up today and scream "No!" to pipelines that destroy sacred land, yell "Time's Up!" to the men and institutions that abuse women, and cry "Black Lives Matter!" to a legal system whose practices suggest that black bodies are without value. I think about the boycotts and the marches, the hashtags and the signs, and I wonder—is this, too, the way of Jesus?

As I consider this current disruption movement, I run through the scriptural narrative in my mind, hunting for evidence that Jesus was involved in acts of resistance, either by instruction or example. However, despite my hopes to the contrary, I could not come up with one example where Jesus or the disciples held up picket signs or marched in the street. There is no record of a sit-in or die-in at the palace gates in Rome. No calls for the resignation of Caesar or Pilate or the chief priest.

> Can a corrupt throne be allied with you—
> a throne that brings on misery by its decrees?
>
> PSALM 94:20 (NIV)

But we need to recognize that there is a record of protest throughout Scripture and that standing *for* often involves standing *against*. Standing for the poor is standing against greed. Standing for the oppressed is standing against tyranny. Standing for love is standing against hate. Standing for righteousness is standing against evil.

Jesus' entire life was an act of defiance. From the moment of his conception in the womb of a virgin to the day he stepped out of the borrowed tomb, Jesus pushed against custom and concept of law. In walking through Samaria rather than going around it, when talking with a woman at a well, by healing on the Sabbath, and when laying hands on lepers, he embodied what it means to defy.

Jesus penned his protest sign in dirt at the feet of an adulterous woman. He inspired men to climb trees so they could see over the crowds. He disrupted many parties and vandalized the temple. He publicly called out religious leaders and challenged the young ruler who was part of the top one percent. He led a march into the city from the back of a donkey; he led a die-in on the cross on a hill. But his ultimate defiance was of hell and death itself when he rose, with all power, from the dead. In doing so, he freed us to live out lives of resistance. In fact, he commands it through his mandate to love.

So we too choose to live out lives of disruption. We resist. We oppose, and we cry. Like our Savior, we dare to contest hatred and defy evil. And in resurrection power, we stand.

2

And He sat down, called the twelve, and said to them, "If anyone desires to be first, he shall be last of all and servant of all."

Mark 9:35

READING: MARK 9:33-37

Years ago, when I was a much younger woman, I was invited by a friend to a women's celebration at a church in Princeton, New Jersey, where she was to be the guest speaker. I was grateful for the invitation and gladly accepted. We traveled there from Pennsylvania, enjoying great conversation along the way.

When we arrived at the church, we were greeted by church leaders who were specially assigned by the pastor to welcome us. They hurried to grab our bags and lead us inside, scurrying ahead to open doors along the way. We followed them up the stairs to a cheerful private dining room where our hosts quickly hung up our coats and then disappeared. To our surprise, a beautifully displayed breakfast spread, hot and ready, was waiting for us.

Before I knew it, an unexpected thought entered my head: *wow, I could get used to this life!* The words slithered through my mind as I scanned the room and smiled. However, almost immediately, like the disciples on the road to Capernaum, I felt exposed and convicted by the Spirit for experiencing that fleshly pride in my heart. I was also frightened by how quickly and easily my soul lusted after promotion. It was my first taste of that pedestal treatment, and I realized I had surely failed the test.

Jesus' words from Mark 9:35 loomed large: "If anyone desires to be first [in position and power], he shall be last of all and servant of all." I wasn't even the guest of honor at the event but merely her friend. Yet I, like the disciples, was seeking to be first in the kingdom. Instead, Jesus suggests that kingdom greatness does not result from pushing yourself to the front or seeking first place in the line. It's not based on the number of followers we have, who we know, or who may know us. No, kingdom greatness is the result of humble service, of choosing the last and the least.

We are often pursuing the admiration of the crowd, craving the favor of those in power, and chasing recognition or prestige. However, Jesus instructs us not to seek or run after power but rather to come after him. When you get me, he says, you get it all. You come after me by receiving the least of these, not the rich and famous. By serving the orphan, the poor, the widow, the felon, and the refugee. You welcome me by welcoming the stranger and receiving them as your own. You get me, you become great. I am your prestige. I am your greatness. I am your privilege and power. I am your treasure. I am your reward. I am your glory.

> I press toward the goal for the prize of the
> upward call of God in Christ Jesus.
>
> PHILIPPIANS 3:14

I left the worship service that day praying that God would purify my heart and keep me from pride and idolatry. Some twenty years later, like Paul, I am in pursuit of a different prize. I want to take custody of that for which I was taken into custody. I want to get that thing that I was gotten to get, to grab the article that God grabbed me to possess. I want to fulfill his purpose.

Despite the time they spent with him, the disciples were still confused about the nature of Jesus' kingdom. No matter how long we've been on the journey we cannot assume we've arrived. We must be constantly working to forget the wisdom and way of this world and constantly straining to grasp the seemingly foolishness that is the upward call of God in Christ Jesus.

3

MEDICINE TREES

And he showed me a pure river of water of life, clear as crystal,
proceeding from the throne of God and of the Lamb.

Revelation 22:1

READING: PSALM 1

Clean water is a blessing. Where the water flows, the banks of the
river grow green and tangled with trees, and those trees become a
source of food for the animals and wildlife living close by. Cities grow
up around water too. The rivers that flow through, by, and around
them wash our bodies, help us cook our food, and generate the
power that lights up the night.

John, describing his revelation, speaks of a river issuing from the
throne of God, a pure river that runs through the street of God's city.
On both sides of the river grows a tree that bears a different fruit for
each month; its leaves help the healing of the nations.

The prophet Ezekiel also described a river flowing out of the sanctuary (Ezekiel 47:1-12). On the banks of that river grow many trees
as well. The river flows eastward into the desert and out to the sea,

bringing healing to the multitude of creatures that swim within. And the trees that grow beside that river likewise produce fruit for food and leaves for medicine.

Meditating on these images, I am reminded of other trees and rivers of water described by David. These trees have no bark or branches but are the trees of godly people, such as the person who delights in the law of the Lord and meditates on it day and night. David writes that the person shall be like a tree planted by the rivers of water, bringing forth fruit in season, and whose leaf shall not wither—whatever they do shall prosper.

Several years ago, my family and I were living in the middle of the popular, southern city Atlanta during a drought. As days rolled into months and months turned into the better part of a year, I watched this "city in the forest" dry up and turn brown. Crops withered, grass died, and the water level of our favorite lake fell dangerously low. Mandatory restrictions were put in place throughout the state in an effort to preserve this precious resource that we had all taken for granted until then.

> Hungry and thirsty,
> Their soul fainted in them.
> Then they cried out to the Lord in their trouble,
> *And* He delivered them out of their distresses.
>
> PSALM 107:5-6

God, by his grace, has given us his Spirit—a stream in the desert, a well springing up into life. Yet time and again, I run past that stream. Pouring myself out every day, I fail to draw from that well until my buckets are nearly empty, my lips are dry and cracked, and my soul is faint and withered.

But when I come into the sanctuary to worship or come before the throne of God in prayer, there I find a river of water flowing from the mouth of God. If I drink from that spring and let it wash over me, I am renewed. I am cleansed. I am quenched. If I stay long enough, drink deep enough, and come often enough, that water will produce the fruit of love, peace, joy, patience, goodness, faithfulness, and self-control in my life. This righteous character becomes food for those around me and water for those in desert places.

Healthy trees also produce leaves. The leaves of the righteous are not grown to adorn the sanctuary or decorate the tree but instead to bring healing to the nations. We are sent to where there is sickness. We are planted in the places of pain to draw out the poisons of corruption, reset the limbs of broken systems, and strengthen the impoverished and oppressed.

From time to time we will enter periods of drought when the rains of relationships may fail. In the heat of adversity, the water lines of health and strength can drop dangerously low. Pools of resource sometimes dry up all together. However, despite these harsh conditions and times of drought, we have been assured that our leaves shall not wither. For our roots are nourished by the river that flows from the throne of God.

4

Then Jesus said to them, "Follow Me, and I will make you become fishers of men." They immediately left their nets and followed Him.

Mark 1:17-18

READING: MARK 1:16-20

In the socially conscious, young, evangelical circles where my husband and I have spent our recent years, environmental concerns have reshaped the norms of gift giving. Rather than spend large amounts of money on new and often useless items, some have adopted the practice of repurposing old things. Pinterest ideas for do-it-yourself presents and services are shared and "liked" with fervor. Baking, crafting, and self-made service coupons are given with pride, and the dollars saved are donated to worthwhile causes and the needs of those abroad. (Of course, for some of us this is not new. We grew up with similar practices born out of necessity with "donated" dollars going to General Electric and our gas company rather than some charity overseas.)

Repurposing begins with thinking differently about how we do or use something. Yielding ourselves to the lordship of Christ is about allowing him to do what sometimes looks like a repurposing of us. We spend countless hours in anxious prayer, desperately trying to discern the will of God for our lives. Then, unclear and unsure, we make what appears to be the most sensible decision and decide . . . to enroll in seminary. Surely there God will reveal the much talked about "plan" that he has for my life! Sometimes the Spirit of God does lead us down this path, but for many it is a rather expensive form of career exploration.

The men and women that were called to follow Jesus came to him with all that they were and all that they knew, and Jesus took that and repurposed it for the glory of God and the benefit of his kingdom. Most often, when Jesus calls us from our boats and nets, he does not require us to forget all that we know of fishing. However, he often redirects that knowledge and experience toward other purposes. Simon, Andrew, James, and John left the pursuit of profit for the pursuit of souls, but they did not cease to be fishermen. Paul left his Pharisaical pursuit of Jewish law enforcement, but he used his knowledge of Jewish law and history, along with his zeal, persistence, and fearlessness, to share the gospel, plant churches, and train and disciple leaders. God repurposed him, and God is repurposing us.

> As He passed by, He saw Levi the *son* of Alphaeus sitting at the tax office. And He said to him, "Follow Me." So he arose and followed Him.
>
> MARK 2:14

As is true with objects, our transition also begins with rethinking about the gifts and skills we possess. You may be called to leave a job but not necessarily a profession. For our God, who knows the end from the beginning, takes our time of "preparation" spent waitressing, gang-banging, getting a college degree, parenting, coffee making, landscaping, working in a lab, teaching, nursing, or answering customer service calls and repurposes our lives to bring the good news of redemption, salvation, and justice to many. For some that path includes a seminary degree; for others it means getting their training on the street and in the barrios, in a church or prison cell.

The question is: On the day Jesus comes strolling down the shore of your everyday life with that all-important invitation, "Come after me," will you be willing to accept the redirection? Will you walk away from what you decided to do in order to become the gift that you are called to be?

5

REVELATION

For I consider [from the standpoint of faith] that the sufferings
of the present life are not worthy to be compared with the
glory that is about to be revealed to us *and* in us!

Romans 8:18 (AMP)

READING: ROMANS 8:18-25

As an educator, creator, and director of leadership programs, I spend a
lot of time talking to people, particularly youth, about purpose. Purpose
is the reason for which something exists or is done, made, or used.

I often ask the question, "Why are you here? Here on earth, at this
moment in time, in this place?" This is where adults will look off into
the distance or drop their eyes to the floor in thought. When adults
respond, if they respond, they speak in hushed and somber tones,
choosing their words carefully. Youth just stare at me with squinted
eyes under crinkled brows before sighing and responding "I don't
know" with a shrug.

It's okay that we struggle with that question. I think we should, as
believers, since a lot is riding on that answer.

> For [even the whole] creation [all nature] waits
> eagerly for the children of God to be revealed.
>
> ROMANS 8:19 (AMP)

Somewhere around 2010, gender reveal parties became a thing. An expectant mom or couple hosts a party dripping with pink and blue decorations for their friends and family members. Then, in some dramatic fashion and with much celebration and cake, the gender of the coming child is revealed. Scripture seems to indicate that there's another reveal for which the whole world is waiting with expectation: the revelation of the children of God. Even nature, all of creation, is subject to this frustration, groaning in pain while waiting for the children of God to be revealed to a hurting and desperate world—waiting for us to be whom we were created to be so that the world might be freed from its bondage to death into glorious freedom.

Think about that. What if the waves are tossing, the trees are bending, the volcanos are erupting, and the earth is shaking as it waits in tension for us to get a clue to who God is, a clue to who we are and why we are here. What's more, we, the sons and daughters of God, who carry the down payment of the Spirit of God within us, are groaning within ourselves—in our fads and trending, scrolling and web surfing, binge watching, binge eating, make-up, make-overs, and endless efforts to make it. We too are groaning with expectation for ourselves to be the people we were created to be in Christ Jesus.

One time in high school, I was sitting at a women's luncheon with my mom. On the table in front of me was a place card with a Scripture reference. I was bored waiting for the program to begin, so I decided to look up my verse:

The Spirit of the Lord God is upon me; because the Lord hath anointed me to preach good tidings unto the meek; he hath sent me to bind up the brokenhearted, to proclaim liberty to the captives, and the opening of the prison to them that are bound;

To proclaim the acceptable year of the Lord, and the day of vengeance of our God; to comfort all that mourn;

To appoint unto them that mourn in Zion, to give unto them beauty for ashes, the oil of joy for mourning, the garment of praise for the spirit of heaviness; that they might be called trees of righteousness, the planting of the Lord, that he might be glorified. (Isaiah 61:1-3 KJV)

I can remember the words leaping off the page at me, disrupting my thoughts and disturbing my spirit. They were more than black ink on white paper. They were a call, a reason for being, a divine purpose. I didn't want to hear it at the time. It didn't make sense. And yet those words set my feet on a path and pointed me in a direction.

The thought that we are somehow involved in, or even more, *critical* to God's great plan of redemption for the world seems ludicrous to many of us. We look at our weak, sinful, and foolish lives and examine our feeble attempts at justice and scoff. And yet God is up to something miraculous, and we have a part in that plan. Rather than hide this mystery in the layers of a cake or the parchment of a hidden scroll, he has chosen to place it within the cracked, clay vessels of our lives and to announce it through the chapped, crooked smiles and halting words of folks like you and me.

As we wait for the final sign of our adoption, the redemption and transformation of our bodies in resurrection, every day brings us closer and closer to that climax. Every day, we become more and more like our Father—with more of his likeness apparent in us. Every day, a little less hateful. Every day, a little more gracious. Every day, a little less complaining, a little more true. God is revealing more of himself to the world through us every day. The more we live into our purpose, answer the call, and walk in the Spirit, the more we become who we were created to be.

6

SMALL TALK

Whoever receives one of these children in My name receives Me.
And whoever receives Me receives not Me, but Him who sent Me.

Mark 9:37 (MEV)

READING: MARK 9:33-37

I used to hate chitchatting at small dinner parties. I'm an introvert, so being thrust into a room full of people I don't know and expected to chat for an indeterminate amount of time used to be particularly grueling. Most challenging of all was the dreaded question, "What do you do?"

It always felt like an examination or mild interrogation. Conversation in the small circle halted, waiting for my answer, and I imagined a spotlight being shined in my eyes. I pictured a large clock appearing on the far wall, with a red second-hand marking time. The room around me seemed to go dark, and dozens of eyes stared searchingly at mine as a bead of sweat ran slowly down the side of my face. What to say . . . what to say . . . what to say? Eventually, I'd rattle off what felt like some lame answer and watch as the inquirers lost interest and turned away. The lights would come up, the conversation would move on, and I'd die just a little inside.

I do leadership development with urban children, youth, and youth leaders—huge in the kingdom of God, unimpressive here on earth to most people. I was playing the comparison game, and my life and work never seemed as amazing and awe-inspiring as everyone else's. I knew I was doing something important, but without a fancy title or a well-known company name, it always felt small.

> And he sat down and called the twelve and said to them, "If any of you desire to be first, the same shall be last of all and servant of all."
>
> MARK 9:35 (DT)

Jesus' disciples were also seeking fancy titles, an uptown address, or an important post in this new ruler's administration. They wanted to be first in his kingdom, perhaps because they admired the privilege of the powerful in their line of view. They were seeking to have favor with Jesus in order to obtain status or promotion and recognition in the eyes of men.

The way we find significance is not by the accumulation of degrees, or "likes," or titles. It's also not found in the cloud of dust we kick up in a flurry of activity. No, greatness is achieved, Jesus says, by accepting the position of servant. And there is no competition for this position. It is the inheritance of the children of God. In his second letter to the Corinthians, Paul writes that those who commend themselves, or measure themselves, or compare themselves lack wisdom and behave like fools. We do not find our value, worth, or security in the titles we possess or in our tiny sphere of earthly power but rather in the fact and privilege that we are the Lord's.

Can you imagine asking the Prince of Wales, "So, what do you do?" The eyes in the room would not fall on him but on the apparently ignorant person who failed to recognize the heir to the throne of England. I suppose if pressed, the Prince might respond, "Depends on the day." For of course he spends his days representing the throne in affairs of state as the royal heir. Such is *our* task, and it is enough.

That means that on some days I'm a nonprofit program director, but other days I'm a concerned neighbor or friend. Sometimes I'm a struggling mother, wading through the chaos of parenting in a technological age. Other days I'm a small, persistent voice, writing and preaching to stir and challenge a reluctant church. I have discovered over the years that more important than what I do is who I am. What I do changes as God assigns and reassigns me, as I grow up and grow older and evolve. But *who I am* is constant—a child of the Most High God. That bears no shame and could never be considered small.

7

THROUGH BLINDNESS AND GRAVECLOTHES

And when we all had fallen to the ground,
I heard a voice speaking to me.

Acts 26:14

READING: ACTS 26:9-15

Though conversion may be pinpointed to a moment, salvation is a process that continues over a lifetime. I am still being saved from old ways of thinking and behaving and am coming to new under-standings, to new life.

Even the transition from death to life is sometimes progressive. Saul, though converted in a flash of light on the Damascus road, still had to travel from spiritual and physical blindness to sight. And Paul continued to grow and receive revelation throughout his life.

In Mark 8:22-25, Jesus is introduced to a blind man in Bethsaida who is looking for healing. The scripture says that the man asked Jesus to touch him but instead Jesus took him by the hand, led him out of town, put spit on his eyes, laid his hands on him, asked him a question, touched him again, and made him look up—only then did the man see clearly. Sometimes change is instantaneous. Most often, though, it's a process.

In this journey of justice and faith, we find ourselves or meet people like us who are in this growth process called salvation. Our tendency is to grow impatient while mumbling, "When will I ever get this right?" or "Is she still doing that?" or "Will things ever change?" We want or expect Jesus to just touch us and be done with it: "Shazam! You're healed!" But instead, Jesus is walking us through a step-by-step process of deliverance that may be neither quick nor simple nor understood—but at the end, there is clarity and salvation. Perhaps salvation itself is not simply a predetermined destination but rather the course you travel to get there. We are being shaped as much by the noes, delays, and slammed doors as we are by the triumphs and victories. Though our modern, microwave, instant-message society conditions us to the immediate and instantaneous, God is not bound by time.

Whether our focus is individuals, systems, or ourselves, it is important to remember that the work of transitioning from death to life is the Lord's, and the timetable is his and his alone. We prepare the soil, plant the seed, cover and water it, and wait. But the process of moving from seed to food, or from death to resurrection, is divine and cannot be rushed or manipulated by us, no matter how hard we work or how badly we want it.

> Jesus said to her, "Did I not say to you that if you would believe you would see the glory of God?"
>
> JOHN 11:40

Mary longed and worked for the healing of her brother Lazarus, but the God-determined course of his recovery was through death and graveclothes before finally reaching the ultimate healing of resurrection.

Some of us have been praying for the healing of a friend, the salvation of a loved one, the change of a law, or the overturning of a policy. Occasionally we hear stories of charges that were suddenly dropped or tumors that inexplicably disappeared. But more often than not, we must walk through a lengthy trial or fast and pray as a spouse moves through surgery then radiation and chemotherapy. Still, along the way, we hear Jesus whisper as he did to Martha in John 11:40: "Did I not say to you . . ."

We forget that time passed between the cross and the empty tomb, between "it is finished" and "all power is given to me." We forget that we are working out this salvation with fear and trembling on a road that, while long and sometimes bumpy, nevertheless leads to wholeness and new life.

So, if it feels like it's too late, or nothing is happening, or you are still stumbling around in the darkness, don't give up. Choose to trust and wait a while longer. It could be your answer is already in the process. Or perhaps God is just making clay.

PART 2

THE GOAL: CHANGING THE WORLD

"SHALOM"

SUNG BY URBAN DOXOLOGY

8

Then the seventy returned with joy, saying, "Lord, even
the demons are subject to us in Your name."

Luke 10:17

READING: LUKE 10:1-9, 17-20

Sometimes our successes can be more devastating than our failures.
We fight, strain, and struggle in pursuit of something or someone that
looks to be good, and after days or months or years, we obtain it.
Dancing and singing, we throw up our arms in triumph. We close our
eyes and sigh in relieved satisfaction, enjoying the moment and the
smooth, cool weight of the victory we now hold in our hands. We bite
and chew, savoring the sweetness of our success. But when we
open our eyes and look around, we are shocked to discover that the
faces of the people we love most are no longer present in the
cheering crowds. The place where we stand is foreign or unfamiliar,
and the reflection in the mirror seems to be not our own.

You stepped into this work to do some good and make a difference, to bring the love of Jesus and the hope of glory to the poor

and broken, those held captive or the oppressed. You read a verse or heard a sermon, and a burning started in your heart. So with zeal and faith you jumped into it with "nothing to lose but our chains."[1] You joined a march or wrote a letter. You made some calls or organized a meeting. And the next thing you knew, there were calendars and microphones and interviews and invitations. You started doing things you didn't used to do, using words you wouldn't normally say. You got a lot less sleep and drank a lot more coffee. You talked more and prayed less, but your Twitter followers grew.

> The harvest truly is great, but the labourers are few: pray ye therefore the Lord of the harvest, that he would send forth labourers into his harvest.
>
> LUKE 10:2 (KJV)

It's easy to get swept away in the heat of it all. These days there is no shortage of issues to address and no lack of battles to fight. But if we're not careful, we can easily lose sight of the named opponent and the purpose of battle in relation to the war. And sometimes, we can even lose ourselves.

The disciples had grown in number. Some seventy would be sent out as a regional advance team to prepare each city for the coming of Christ. They were given instructions as to what to expect on the trip, what to take, and what they were to say and do. Implicit in these instructions was the fact that the disciples would now possess certain special abilities, which included miraculous healing and the power to bless and even curse. They could pack lightly because in many cities they would discover that lodging and food were provided for them.

However, most importantly, they were being sent with a message: the kingdom of God has come near in the person of Jesus Christ.

Perhaps the new disciples, much like many of us, were a little nervous but mostly excited to be used in service to Christ. But before long, they seemed to get caught up in the short-term success of the mission, their newfound friends, and their abilities that included power over demonic spirits. Likewise, with our rally crowd numbers, signatures on electronic petitions, Instagram and Twitter followers, or speaking invites and publishing contracts, we rejoice that the demonic systems of our world appear to be subject to us in some large or small way.

Then the voice of God reminds us that he saw Satan himself fall from heaven a long time ago, and of course, God has power over all of our power. The trophies that we're clutching belong to him, and the sweetness we taste in our mouths is from a fruit given, not earned.

So while it is fine to celebrate the victories over the systemic evils of one country on one continent of one small planet of the universe, we must not lose sight of the greater triumph. We have been grafted into the family of the Lord of all creation and sent ahead to proclaim the news of his return so that we can invite and prepare a people for his kingdom.

9

BIG SHOES

Now thanks be unto God, which always causeth
us to triumph in Christ, and maketh manifest the
savour of his knowledge by us in every place.

2 Corinthians 2:14 (KJV)

READING: 2 CORINTHIANS 2:14-17

God always causes us to triumph. That's a *big* statement. I don't
know about you, but most days I feel far less than triumphant—and
some days, I feel just a hair above failure. My call and my purpose
on most days feels far too big for me. I imagine myself like a small
child, shuffling through the world in daddy's shoes that are about five
times my size. I have to swing my arms and strain my legs just to
keep my feet inside the shoes. On most days, I feel that my stumbling, slow progress is apparent to all.

I want to think that it was different for Paul. I mean, he's the writer
of most of the New Testament. Of course he felt triumphant. He was
running around laying hands on folks, setting up churches, and
writing really long, inspiring letters. And then he had the whole

Damascus-road-voice-from-heaven experience to boot (Acts 9). Yes, I want to believe that it was easy for Paul, that he was some special guy with super spiritual powers that of course made him triumphant. I want to believe that narrative, though there is much to suggest otherwise, because then I can more easily explain why that is not my general experience—because after all, I'm just . . . me.

I stay up too late and struggle out of bed in the morning. My knees hurt, and I can never get my hair right two days in a row. I'm impatient and critical, and I can seldom find my phone, even when it's in my hand! There are a ton of reasons why I am unqualified to do what God has called me to do. And yet he calls. And yet the Spirit whispers. And yet he sends me—and perhaps he sends you too.

For God, the creator of the universe, has chosen to reveal himself in every place through us. And despite our unflattering self-assessments, to him we are a sweet fragrance of Christ that he sends to both the saved and the lost. The trouble is that although for some we bring the scent of life, like the smell of fresh bread hot from the oven, for others we bring the stench of death, like a smelly animal carcass in the midsummer heat. For one, we are a reminder of the Father, like a welcomed note from home. For the other, we are a sickening cloud exposing failures, an offensive odor causing one to grimace and turn away.

> To the one *we are* the aroma of death *leading* to death, and to the other the aroma of life *leading* to life. And who *is* sufficient for these things?
>
> 2 CORINTHIANS 2:16

We seesaw between this love and rejection, feeling inadequate and unequipped, questioning the appointment, and time and again we are on the verge of walking away. But then he reminds us of his preordained triumph, and we are still. In Christ, we are sufficient. Sufficient simply means adequate for the purpose. Yeah, I know. Bent and ordinary, plain and imperfect, we are enough. I think it's called grace.

At the end of a busy day I sometimes lie in bed running through the conversations and interactions of that day in my mind. At times I groan out loud and grimace as I reflect on it, wishing desperately that I had chosen different words or said something more or nothing at all. I sigh and wish I were better at it all: friendship, leadership, parenting, and peace. Despite the bright moments of joy and success, we often choose to dwell on the dark clouds of anger, misunderstandings, and fear. When I whine and point out what appears to be an enormous chasm between who I am and who I am called to be, God offers a gentle reminder that, while he chooses to use me, it's not about me.

By grace we have been made sufficient: adequate for the purpose. And so, in the too-big shoes of our Father, I shuffle on.

10

DECISIONS, DECISIONS

Now the serpent was more cunning than any beast
of the field which the Lord God had made.

Genesis 3:1

READING: GENESIS 3:1-7

It was early in the new year when my devotion time led me back to Genesis, back to the beginning where the man and his wife were in the garden with God, naked and unashamed. I love finding new insights in old, familiar passages, and once again the text did not disappoint. I read the dialogue between the woman and the serpent, the familiar exchange we have heard time and again.

The conversation begins innocently enough with a question from the serpent to the woman: "Did God really say . . . ?" The serpent, described as more cunning than any of the other wild animals that God made, places his suggestion in question form, and it is enough to lead the woman to reexamine what until now she had simply accepted as true. Sensing the open door, the serpent moves quickly, turning the question into the lie. I can picture him rolling his eyes, shaking his head, and exaggerating a chuckle as he hisses, "You will not certainly die. . . . For God knows that when you eat from it your eyes will be opened, and you will be like God, knowing good and evil" (Genesis 3:4-5 NIV).

Hearing this story time and again, from the lectern and the pulpit, I always thought that everything was fine until Adam and Eve took a bite of that fruit. The bite, the act itself, was where it all fell apart. They disobeyed God, and sin entered the world. However, now I suspect that the first sin was not the *act* of disobedience but rather the *decision* to disobey. The point of decision is always where rebellion first occurs. It is here that we question God's law and his right to require it of us. We scrutinize his motives, which attacks his nature or, at the very least, calls it into question. We challenge his omniscience and resist his sovereignty, for it takes all of this to choose to disobey.

> For *as* the heavens are higher than the earth,
> So are My ways higher than your ways,
> And My thoughts than your thoughts.
>
> ISAIAH 55:9

While walking the path of justice and out in the world doing good, we are sometimes confronted with dark choices disguised as "opportunities." We are tempted to argue ends over means, to justify, rationalize, and compromise, to surrender to the base and the questionable. Questions arise when Satan presents an opposing position or outcome to what God has said: "You will not certainly die."

It is then that we begin to reason with ourselves: *Well, after all, the tree does have fruit on it. What other purpose does it have if not for food?! And it looks so good. And it will be good for me, making me wise. What harm can eating one piece do? Just . . . one . . . bite . . .*

But immediately there is shame, guilt, fear, and an attempt to brush over it, to cover up or hide ourselves from God. However, here is the beautiful irony. God does not move away from us. We—like Adam, Eve, Cain, and the countless men and women who came after—move away from him. The presence of the one true and living God comes for us, calling us by name, and we hide among the trees of our busyness in fear and disbelief. Yet God still and always pursues us.

As we step timidly across the threshold of a new year, a new job, or a new relationship, we may be tempted to quickly construct our own fig-leaf resolutions in a feeble attempt to cover the mistakes of the past. But in fasting and prayer, in solitude and stillness, we are reminded that the sacrifice demanded for our sin has been met in Christ. We can hear the lie in the enemy's questions and, rather than question God's motives, acknowledge the selfish desires of our own hearts. And, by the power of the Spirit, we can *decide* to trust not only in God's will concerning justice but also in his way to accomplish it. Then there is no condemnation, no compromise or disobedience, no need to cover ourselves and hide. No, instead, we can come boldly before him, like little children, naked and un-ashamed once again.

11

AVOIDING BURNOUT

And this they did, not as we hoped, but first gave their own
selves to the Lord, and unto us by the will of God.

2 Corinthians 8:5 (KJV)

READING: 2 CORINTHIANS 8:1-15

I always know when I'm spiritually dehydrated. I'm tired and short-tempered, easily stressed, and feeling overworked. I snap at my children, resent friends and family, and am generally annoyed by the people I say I am called to serve. In my dreams, I see myself as drowning. Wide awake, I am overwhelmed. And then, as if a divine finger is tapping my shoulder, I recognize this familiar place and stop. I am doing it again: working in my own strength and striving in my own power to do what only God can do. I am giving myself to others and becoming angry that they seem ungrateful, when instead I should be giving myself to him.

Emptying myself before the Father is a necessary and recurring step in my discipleship journey. Of my own free will, I approach the altar of God. I lay down all of me as a yielded sacrifice. My body, my mind, my gifts and talents, my possessions, my time, my relationships, my future, my hopes and dreams and desires and imagination—I lay it all at his feet in response to the immense gift of life I have received from him. It is not until I am spent, completely empty of myself, that I am ready to serve others.

We cannot serve from our own wealth, no matter how great, for it will soon be depleted. If we attempt to give to others out of our own supply, our generosity can quickly deteriorate into paternalism, or become tainted by the impure motives of power and control, or weighted with the expectation of reciprocity. No, we must give out of the resources of heaven that we access when we enter the quiet space of worship and prayer—the holy of holies. There, as we stand before the throne of his greatness, we remember the truth. Then we can open our empty hands, heart, and mind before him and be filled.

> And God is able to make all grace abound toward you; that ye, always having all sufficiency in all things, may abound to every good work.
>
> 2 CORINTHIANS 9:8 (KJV)

Over the years we are often prompted to open our lives to others, to make room in our homes, work, or schedules for strangers and friends. We share time and family, business contacts and date nights, holidays and influence, speaker platforms and food. We move through the world like I imagine the disciples waded through the hungry crowds, marveling at God's provision. We close our eyes in prayer over bread crumbs and scraps of fish. He sends us out with hands and baskets nearly empty. Our bodies get tired and our feet grow sore from the journey. Yet moving at his command, every step taken and every item shared brings God-given grace. And we soon realize we have even more to give.

When we begin at empty, we are forced to work from God's supply, according to his timetable and at his pace. We are more often unseen and may go unappreciated, but we are seldom burned out. Instead we are emptied again and again, forced to return to our source to be refilled with his grace and power and sustained by his infinite love. When we first give our whole selves to him without coercion, then our sacrifices, no matter how great or how many, seem quite small.

12

HIGH STEPPING

Because strait is the gate, and narrow is the way, which
leadeth unto life, and few there be that find it.

Matthew 7:14 (KJV)

READING: MATTHEW 7:13-28

On a recent flight home from Atlanta to Portland, I had a privileged
view out my husband's window. Outside the sky appeared as a floor,
covered by a white, wooly blanket that stretched for miles and disappeared into the sunset on the horizon. The clouds, thick and tight
and twisted close together like row after row of stitches, resembled
a cable-knit sweater. I had the strong desire to step outside the
heavy door of the plane and stroll across them with bare feet.

My eyes convinced me the clouds were solid and could easily
hold my weight, that I wouldn't drop through and disappear into the
gray dusk below, and that the golden ribbon of sky in the distance
was just a short walk to the south.

> There is a way *that seems* right to a man,
> But its end *is* the way of death.
>
> PROVERBS 14:12

The narrow way of righteousness and faith can appear hard, dim, and foolish to the masses while the wide road of compromise looks smooth and bathed in light. Sometimes choosing the narrow way means turning down the nicer house by the golf course and opting instead for the smaller fixer-upper on the corner of a dimly lit, dead-end street because that street is filled with children and families with few opportunities. Other times it's choosing the pay cut over the pay raise or electing to preach to forgotten men in an obscure prison chapel over the well-dressed congregants of a mainline church. It may mean becoming a public defender rather than having your name on the wall of a well-known firm, or investing your wealth in the life of an urban youth instead of the stock market. The narrow road is strewn with self-denial and often feels rocky and mostly uphill. The wide road seems to be covered with a carpet of fluffy, cool goodness that slants on a downgrade. *I can still do well on that path,* we tell ourselves. *I can get there faster and with less expense. I can help more people and make fewer enemies. Everyone else goes that way. The laws of gravity are outdated. I can step out of this plane and touch the sun!*

But we can't change the world without changing ourselves. The crowded road of least resistance leads only to shame and disappointment. The narrow road presses in on us, compelling us to adjust our perspective, gait, and pace. It forces us to wrestle with our pride and confront our impatience, and it brings us face-to-face with our insecurities. But along that narrow path, we shake off doubts and fears, and we grow ever stronger. There are no shortcuts or cliché bypasses. There is just through—eyes ahead and feet to concrete.

So despite the beautiful temptation outside my window, I leaned back in my middle seat and settled in for the long flight home. Occasionally during my journey, I sighed and squirmed and checked the time because it felt like we were hardly moving and like the trip would never end. But the flight tracker clocked us at 586 miles per hour and ever closer to our goal. Sometimes over the course of this journey, in the fulfillment of this commitment to call, the narrow path seems to demand too much, and the wide path seems a more sensible option. But then too my senses deceive me. For the word is true, and time and experience have repeatedly shown that faithful obedience is the only road that leads to life. Lord, help us to find it daily.

13

WELLS AND WATERPOTS

If you knew the gift of God, and who it is who says
to you, "Give Me a drink," you would have asked
Him, and He would have given you living water.

John 4:10

READING: JOHN 4:1-14

Engaging in the work of the kingdom can be tricky. We are often sent into places and situations without a full awareness of our role. The assumption quite often, especially if you are coming from a place of privilege, is that you are going to give. After all, we appear to be the ones with the resources, whether that be money, degreed education, or time. Those "being served" have little to nothing, so it is reasonable, understandable, and therefore likely . . . to us . . . that we are there to give.

We ask questions like, "Where can God best use me?" and, "What would you have me to do?" And though I've seen many people return from service projects or mission trips and humbly declare before admiring crowds how "we received far more than we gave,"

I've never heard anyone elaborate on exactly what was learned, gained, or received. It is important to acknowledge that we arrive at most places and situations just like the Samaritan woman—hot, parched, empty, and in search of water.

Thankfully, Jesus shows up to quench our thirst, though we often don't recognize him. Sometimes Jesus is disguised as a homeless man in the soup kitchen line or a woman on the pew in the prison chapel. Perhaps he's the teen we drive to the courthouse in the early morning hours or the teary-eyed mother staring back at us from the other side of the government desk. Some days he looks like the child in ill-fitting clothes in our classroom and at other times like an Israelite Jew covered in dust and sweat at a well. If we get stuck on the outward appearance, we can miss the gift of God standing right in front of us. If we get distracted by what he's asking for, we can miss the wealth of what he came to give.

> But whoever drinks of the water that I shall give him will never thirst. But the water that I shall give him will become in him a fountain of water springing up into everlasting life.
>
> JOHN 4:14

One of the most powerful interactions I ever had was with a homeless man I met in Atlanta. He lived off the University Avenue exit ramp of Interstate 75/85. I would pass him every day on my way home from work as I waited at the stoplight at the end of the ramp. His clothes were filthy, his blond hair long and matted, and like many others, he held a cardboard sign asking for help.

On most days as I passed, I did what many good, American Christians do. I pretended not to see him and his sign. I busied myself with the radio or checked out my nails while waiting anxiously for the light to turn green. However, on one particularly hard day in my nonprofit life, I did not have to pretend. I was lost in my thoughts, weary with discouragement, and fighting back tears when I realized that someone was talking to me. It was a clear, fall day, so my window was down. I turned my head to find the man looking straight at me.

"I'm sorry, what did you say?" I muttered.

"It's going to be alright," I heard him respond.

And for the first time I looked past the dirt and the hair and found kind, warm, caring eyes. I don't know if it was the way he said it or the way he looked at me, but in that moment I believed him and felt better.

"What is your name?" I heard myself say quite unexpectedly, and he replied, "Michael." I thanked him. The light changed from red to green. I smiled at Michael and slowly drove away.

We are often like the Samaritan woman, standing before Jesus. In his presence we spout off claims of our historical ownership of the well. We stand with pride in our knowledge of the local customs and possession of the waterpots. And Jesus stands before us, hands empty yet full of the living water we need to bring us new life. We may feel uncomfortable in his gaze and exposed by his questions. But if we will ourselves to stay in the conversation and adjust our posture from giving to receiving, our eyes may be opened to see the Christ. Only then may we become partners with the Spirit, inviting and helping others to see him as well.

14

ROCKS AND RECORD KEEPERS

When Jesus had raised Himself up and saw no one but the woman, He said to her, "Woman, where are those accusers of yours? Has no one condemned you?"

John 8:10

READING: JOHN 8:1-11

John's account tells us that Jesus was in the temple teaching when the religious leaders and record keepers brought him a woman caught in the act of adultery. In front of the crowd, they began to question Jesus as to how they should respond to the woman and her sin. They reminded him what the law required: public execution. Of course, the question posed was not really about the woman but instead was a test of the heart of the person who was being questioned.

Almost every day we too are presented with this same test. How do we respond to the "law breakers" in light of the teachings and example of Christ? Today the question comes to us from the so-called religious leaders in our lives, and sometimes that religious leader is us. Individuals, churches, and institutions are wrestling with an assortment of men, women, and even systems that have been caught in acts that conflict with righteous law. How do we, as people of faith and justice, respond?

Interestingly, Jesus does not get involved in a political debate or present a theological case. He simply stoops down and writes something on the ground. In this moment, so heavy with accusation and future implication, Jesus' first response is silence. Why does he pause? To gather his thoughts? To play for a time in the sand? Perhaps he pauses to pray, to receive instruction from the Father. Perhaps he wants to give the accusers time to repent or change their minds, or to give others an opportunity to respond or intervene. Perhaps he made a note of where he stopped in the lesson he'd been teaching. We only know that he paused, and they waited.

The question is put to us as well, time and time again, and the watching world is waiting for our reply. How do we respond to the real estate developers crafting plans for gentrification? What do we say about the politicians who continuously press us toward war? How do we engage the gay coworker at the office, the police officers defending the most recent shootings, or the neighbor with the opposing political party's sticker on their car?

In our modern vernacular, Jesus' response is a mic drop. The reminder and awareness of the religious leaders' own sin turned their anger and evil intentions to shame, and one by one, they dropped their rocks and left. Jesus' answer teaches us again that only a sinless person can rightfully condemn another. He does not condone.

He does not excuse. He simply points out that we are all likewise guilty. The reminder of this truth sets the accused woman free.

> So when they continued asking Him, He raised Himself up and said to them, "He who is without sin among you, let him throw a stone at her first." And again He stooped down and wrote on the ground.
>
> JOHN 8:7-8

As we move through the world confronting evil systems, we undoubtedly will face the people that construct and support them. How we respond to those who are "caught in the act" is also important. As with Jesus, the question may be posed to us publicly, before God and a crowd of witnesses, to test us against the gospel of love and grace that we preach. If we feel called to point out the sins of others, we must never forget that we are all likewise guilty. To point out sin as a fellow sinner is an entirely different posture. We are not sent to condemn but to redeem. It is the forgiveness and grace of the only righteous one that brings salvation. Preaching the gospel and doing justice isn't about spouting laws, it's about sharing stories—our stories of guilt, forgiveness, and grace.

PART 3

THE MEANS: NEW BIRTH

"ABIDE IN ME"

SUNG BY URBAN DOXOLOGY

15

BEGIN AGAIN

And all things are of God, who hath reconciled us to himself by Jesus Christ, and hath given to us the ministry of reconciliation.

2 Corinthians 5:18 (KJV)

READING: 2 CORINTHIANS 5:14-21

I think God likes do-overs. A do-over is a reset, a reboot, a chance to go back to the beginning and start again fresh. When things are going downhill fast, from bad to worse, with increasingly little chance of recovery, a decision is made to start again rather than give up and walk away.

Noah and the ark were a do-over. Jesus' death and resurrection are a do-over. Winter and then spring, night and then morning, baptism and rebirth—salvation—are total do-overs. Each is another chance to start again with a clean slate, fresh eyes, and new hope.

Reconciliation is the pathway to a relational do-over. As a child, I remember my parents' marriage as constant turmoil, with lots of arguing, anger, and tension. Several times my mother packed up and left with me in tow. Then, after some days or a week (and once, even after a year), we would go back, and she and my dad would reconcile. For them that meant again living under the same roof and resuming life together as it had been. We lived in that cycle of anger, explosion, separation, and reconciliation for much of my childhood.

> Therefore, if anyone *is* in Christ, *he is* a
> new creation; old things have passed away;
> behold, all things have become new.
>
> 2 CORINTHIANS 5:17

When God speaks of reconciliation, I believe he has something more in mind. Salvation doesn't bring us back to God so that we can exchange stiff, awkward hugs, mumble apologies, and then carry on with our lives as we previously knew them. God's reconciliation begins with a winter, a nighttime, a death that serves to baptize us into something new. Our old ways of relating to God and to one another have to pass away.

We cannot hope to end the evils of racism, poverty, war, and oppression unless we are willing to let go and die to some things. Reconciliation is then not an end but a jumping off point into something new and more beautiful. It is the beginning of new ways of thinking and speaking to and about one another, new ways of interacting and working together. Reconciliation is the platform on which we stand together surveying the possibilities of what could be, the launching pad into a new and more fruitful life. It begins with the awareness that though we were enemies to God, God now, through Christ, has given us a clean slate—not counting our past sin against us but accepting us as sons and daughters and working with and through us to love the world. It is completed as we extend this grace to others.

> Now then, we are ambassadors for Christ, as though God were pleading through us: we implore *you* on Christ's behalf, be reconciled to God.
>
> 2 CORINTHIANS 5:20

16

CHANGE OF PLANS

Immediately there fell from his eyes *something* like scales, and
he received his sight at once; and he arose and was baptized.

Acts 9:18

READING: ACTS 9:1-18

His name was Saul of the well-known city Tarsus in south-central
Turkey. He was a young up-and-comer, well into his life plan: Completed his Ivy League education. Hired and promoted to a place of
power in his chosen career. Politically connected and well known.
And he was on a mission, of his own choosing, to rid his country of
"those" people.

For this reason, Saul sets out for the town of Damascus all fired
up and determined. However, just before reaching his destination,
he is intercepted by the living God. As a result of this encounter, he
is changed.

The first indication of this change is the abandonment of his plans
and instead the asking of a profound question: "Lord, what will you
have me do?" This is the true evidence of conversion. It is the giving

up of *my* plans, *my* goals, and *my* dreams, the giving over of *my* life and the surrender of *my* will to the divine will of another. For it is not enough to simply call him "Lord." Responding to him as Lord means walking in obedience to his instruction and doing things his way. The Lord answers Saul's question not with a new five- or ten-year plan but with a simple one-step instruction. And perhaps in confusion or frustration, afraid or amazed, Saul obeys. Assisted by some temporary blindness, he spends the next three days fasting and waiting.

Like Saul, we may have had plans for our lives before and even after coming to Christ. We thought about a wedding day, the university we'd attend, where we would live, the vacations we'd take, the business we'd start, or the type of car we'd drive. For me, it was musical theater. I signed up and auditioned for many church productions and school plays. My parents sacrificed hard-earned dollars for my piano and dance lessons. From age three to well past college, I sang in some choir, ensemble, or praise team. Theater was my plan for me—but God had another.

In my early twenties, I was on a solitary walk in the woods during a break while attending a mission retreat, and I had my own Damascus Road experience. Before long, I came to a fork in the path, and the Spirit of God posed a question: "Donna, are you willing to be made poor so that others might be made rich?"

I don't know how long I stood at that fork, heart pounding, eyes closed, trying to summon the courage and will to answer. But eventually, with my voice shaking and tears falling, I whispered, "Yes, Lord."

I don't understand how, but I knew in that moment that the trajectory of my life had changed. I had chosen more than a path. I had chosen him, over my plans, over myself. Years before, as a child, I had invited Jesus into my heart, but that day in the woods, I surrendered my life.

As challenging as it may be to come to terms with our own conversion, it is sometimes even harder to believe in the power of God to transform another, especially an enemy. When the Lord speaks to Ananias concerning Saul, Ananias is less than eager to believe it. He responds the way we might respond to God sending us to minister to a member of ISIS or the KKK. I imagine that there was more than a little reluctance in Ananias's heart as he headed toward Straight Street. Yet, acknowledging him as Lord, Ananias obeys, not only putting his hands on Saul but also calling him "brother." Through that act of obedience, Saul received sight and was baptized.

> But why do you call me, "Lord, Lord," and
> not do the things which I say?
>
> LUKE 6:46

Conversion is more than just a prayer that's prayed in a moment. It is a surrendered will and a yielded vessel throughout a lifetime. It is the giving up and the giving over and the giving in. It is dying daily while becoming more and more alive. It is the miraculous work of God, by his Spirit and for his glory, which none of us deserve and yet into which all of us, regardless of the evil we have done or the sins we have committed, are invited.

Therefore, leaving the discussion of the elementary *principles* of
Christ, let us go on to perfection, not laying again the foundation
of repentance from dead works and of faith toward God.

Hebrews 6:1

READING: HEBREWS 5:12–6:1

Christian conversion is not merely a one-time experience but rather
an ongoing process through which we take on the mind, character,
behavior, and lifestyle of the living Christ. I am a convert ever moving
through conversion or being converted. If I have ceased to change
and grow, I am in spiritual crisis.

When I take my child in for an annual checkup, the doctor often
reviews my child's growth chart with us. This chart is a grid with
points plotted showing where my child's height and weight stand in
relation to previous years and other children of like gender and age.
Lines are drawn that help to connect and highlight my child's growth
from year to year. I wonder—if God were to print out my spiritual
growth chart, would the lines drawn curve gently upward, suggesting

growth and overall health? Would the points plotted indicate that I am moving ever onward toward spiritual maturity? Or have my lines leveled off in recent years or, worse, begun to slope dangerously downward toward spiritual death?

From the moment of conception, our physical bodies are changing and growing. With adequate air, space, and nutrition, we grow and become ever more complex and developed. However, if a child stops growing after birth, there would be reason for alarm. Many of us have spiritual midwives who coaxed us into this new life and may have walked alongside us through spiritual infancy, but from the moment we could walk, talk, and feed ourselves, we were left to find our own way. The goal is not that we merely experience new birth but that, through a continuous process of conversion, we are conformed to the image of Jesus Christ. Conformity to the world is the mark of a spirit and mind no longer moving through conversion.

> Life is more than food, and the body *is more* than clothing.
>
> LUKE 12:23

The American Academy of Pediatrics developed a set of comprehensive health guidelines for well-child care called Bright Futures. Each well-child visit includes age appropriate questions focused on developmental milestones such as nutrition, safety, and emotional well-being. If my child's physical chart suggested a lack of or decline in physical growth, my doctor would ask questions about nutrition and caloric intake. We would review food choices and amounts as well as activity levels and rest patterns, and she would likely make recommendations for change and schedule follow-up visits.

Unfortunately, there is no Kingdom Academy of Discipleship with a published list of "well-child" guidelines. As followers of Jesus, Scripture gives us markers against which we can assess our spiritual growth and well-being. Accountability comes with participation in Christian community. Although there are no spiritual milestones associated with age-specific stages of development, we know that healthy disciples produce love, joy, peace, long-suffering, kindness, goodness, meekness, faith, and self-control—the fruit so desperately needed to confront the ills of our broken world. These virtues address not just what we do but also how we do it. We cannot engage in the demanding work of social justice while stunted or spiritually malnourished.

The Word of God, the Holy Spirit, and the body of Spirit-filled believers are the guides given to help us evaluate our present state of spiritual health for signs of growth or malnourishment and to outline the diet and habits that can be adjusted to bring about healthy change. Though change can often be hard or painful, we can take comfort in the promise that we have been predestined to be conformed to the image of God's Son, that he might be the firstborn among many brothers and sisters (see Romans 8:29).

18

EXCEPT YOU BECOME AS CHILDREN

Truly I say to you, Except you be converted, and become as little
children, you shall not enter into the kingdom of heaven.

Matthew 18:3 (DT)

READING: MATTHEW 18:1-6

If you spend any time observing young children at play, it quickly
becomes apparent that children perceive with the mind and heart—
seeing the invisible, responding to the inaudible, feeling the intangible.[1] They take great care in spooning imaginary food into a
doll's open mouth, ducking behind columns and walls to avoid make-
believe bullets from an unseen enemy, and acting out elaborate
death scenes as they fall into unseen pools of lava on the living
room floor. They are not limited in their thinking by the *shoulds* and
should nots and are not consumed with what "people" will think or
say or what is or is not supposed to be. They are free.

Child*like* is not child-*ish*. *Childishness* is that self-centered thinking
and lifestyle that blocks our gratitude to the mercy and faithfulness of

64

God and closes our hands and hearts to the needs of those around us. Childishness blinds us to injustices that are not our own and to the privilege we daily enjoy. Childishness causes us to shrink with irrational fears and make demands for comforts we don't deserve.

However, *childlikeness* is an altogether different state of being. Childlikeness causes us to think of others, to take bread even from our own mouth to share with a friend. Childlikeness squeals with delight at the simple beauty of nature, dances with joy over the treasures found that money cannot buy, and sobs with heartfelt sorrow over the pain of a neighbor or friend. Most importantly, childlikeness believes what seems impossible to grownups, despite all evidence to the contrary, even to the saving of the soul.

Jesus invites us into this space, this childlike thinking and being. "But, Lord," we say, "how do we make the leap from our hardened adult realism into the innocence of faith? How do we shut our eyes to the deception of the natural and liberate our minds and hearts to the reality of the spirit?" And Jesus responds, "If you abide in My word, you are My disciples indeed. And you shall know the truth, and the truth shall make you free" (John 8:31-32).

As we grow up and older, the pains and challenges of adulthood begin to block out the truth. Disappointment and broken hearts shake the ground beneath our feet. What we once believed to be certain becomes harder and harder to imagine.

In the late '90s, my husband and I relocated to Atlanta to serve with a Christian nonprofit that required us to raise our own support. We married young. Our family was poor. We had three young children and little-to-no savings. The dream of home ownership seemed more like foolish fantasy. Before long, without realizing it, I gave up on the hope of the miraculous, settling instead for the probable, practical, and real. We were grinding every day to change the world and make a difference while fighting every night just to survive. There was no time for childlike thinking. I decided to embrace the facts of our reality and become content.

Fortunately, I later discovered something when we moved into our newly built home: the facts are not the same as the truth. The facts told Mary that her brother Lazarus was dead and decomposing inside the tomb, but the truth was that a live man walked out of the tomb when Jesus, the resurrection and the life, called his name. The facts say that water, composed of two parts hydrogen and one part oxygen, cannot support the weight of a man, but the truth is that Jesus and Peter walked on water. Jesus, who is the way, the truth, and the life, regularly contradicts the facts given to us by the world.

> Therefore whoever humbles himself as this little child is the greatest in the kingdom of heaven.
>
> MATTHEW 18:4

In our busy lives, we must create room for ourselves and others to think without having an answer to every question. We must make space for the heart to dance and laugh and sing without the noise of conflict, and we must allow places for play where the spirit can connect with the God who gave it. We must make space to receive new visions and dream new dreams.

Unlike the body, the soul is not made free by legal or political proclamation. Freedom is the result of the knowledge of the truth—

the truth that we are fearfully and wonderfully made. The truth that we are created in the image of God. The truth that God knows us, chose us, and loves us without condition. That he is with us to protect us and provide whatever is needed so that we shall not want or fear or lose. We are then free to imagine what can be, to create what is not yet, and to run into the unknown fully open to the experience. We can explore the curiosities of life and respond with honesty. We can risk being vulnerable and caring and giving away unrestrained love. We can dare to hope, imagine, and dream. In fact, we have been invited to do so, knowing that our hope will not bring us shame. We can believe in God and do the impossible. We must allow ourselves to be childlike and pursue this transformation, this renewal of mind. For without it we shall never see the kingdom of God.

19

SIMPLE INSTRUCTIONS

Speak unto them, saying, At even ye shall eat flesh,
and in the morning ye shall be filled with bread; and
ye shall know that I am the LORD your God.

Exodus 16:12 (KJV)

READING: EXODUS 16:11-31

At the end of the day, obedience is rest. Rest in God's promises. Rest in God's power. Rest in God's love and commitment to us. It is having faith that he knows the ways we go and is at work to produce the best in and through us.

While the people of Israel were wandering in the desert, God gave them a set of very simple directions: "At twilight you shall eat meat, and in the morning you shall be filled with bread. And you shall know that I *am* the LORD your God" (Exodus 16:12). Simple. Three instructions. Although they had some challenges with the second, their real source of struggle was with the third.

Moses told them to take only what they needed. Don't try to save any. But of course, some seemingly "wise" persons didn't listen and saved their food overnight, waking up to a smelly, rotting mess. Moses told them to gather the bread for six days but not to gather on the seventh. Still, some we-know-better folks ventured out on day seven and came back empty-handed. The funny thing is, God didn't see them as wise or resourceful. He saw them as disobedient. God gave Israel enough bread on the sixth day to meet the needs of the seventh. Likewise, he has given me what I need to obey him. Why do I not?

> Notwithstanding they did not heed Moses. But some of them left part of it until morning, and it bred worms and stank. And Moses was angry with them.
>
> EXODUS 16:20

I think about the areas of my life where I am struggling with obedience, areas where through God's Word, his Spirit, or his people, I have been given clear instruction. But instead I, like Israel, decide to do otherwise. When I am still, quiet, and reflective enough to search for the why, I am confronted with the ugly truth. In this area of my life, I do not believe God. I do not believe that his instructions are right. I do not see how they make sense. I believe that I have a better way. And so I, like Israel, go my own way and fail—or worse, go my own way and succeed in the short term but lose in a more significant, long-term area of my life. I go my own way because in that moment of decision, I have chosen to be in control, to determine my own best interest. I have forgotten or ignored instruction number three: "Know that I am God."

When I allow the Spirit of God to get to the root of that thinking, I discover that my unbelief is not just in God's wisdom or power but also ultimately in his love for me. I am not simply questioning whether or not he *can* take care of me but rather whether or not he will, whether or not he wants to. I am saddened to realize that in doing so I am in fact questioning his nature, the character of God, the very essence of who he is as well as who he is to me. The Holy Spirit exposes me, and I am naked and shamed before him. For if he is not love, he is nothing at all.

The Lord sends down manna into our lives sufficient for our present need. Still we sigh and pace about, wringing our hands in fear. Fretful over what might happen. And again and again God has to remind me. I am God. You are not. My ways and thoughts are higher.

And so, tired and sore from our futile, seventh-day searching, we shuffle home. We go back to our place—as the child, the follower, the servant of the Most High—and find rest. In that place of yielding and concession, we enjoy the manna of God, and the taste of it is like honey in our mouth.

20

SLAVES VERSUS SONS

And a slave does not abide in the house
forever, *but* a son abides forever.

John 8:35

READING: JOHN 8:31-51

Freedom is a strange concept. Most often in the Western world we think of it in terms of freedom from something or someone—freedom from tyranny, freedom from debt, freedom from oppression. More often than not, however, in the upside-down life of the kingdom, we are given freedom *to*.

As children of God and followers of Christ, we are free *to* do good and free to serve, free to give without expecting anything in return. We are free to love even our enemies and free to choose peace over war. Most importantly, we are free to enjoy and employ the grace of God in our lives without the guilt and shackles of the law. Yet we often forfeit this freedom through compromise and indenture ourselves to an unseen master.

Whoever commits sin is a slave of sin.

JOHN 8:34

No matter who we are, it is clear that we have all experienced this form of bondage. Paul writes that all have sinned and come short of the glory of God (Romans 3:23). And if all have sinned, then at some point (perhaps this morning) we have all felt the weight of that servitude. We have all been entangled, held by sin's cords and forced to bow down.

The problem with living so long in bondage is that one can develop a slave mentality. Though free, we continue to live on massa's land and eat massa's food. We make a decision but wait for massa to give a nod of approval, and then we rethink and cast it out when he does not.

Jesus often presents the dichotomy of the slave or servant versus the son. Servants can be thrown out at any time. Servants have no inheritance, but sons remain family and heirs forever. The law produces servants, but grace produces sons. As a servant, I must work to please the master. But as his child, I am made free to respond to the Father's love.

The children of God recognize the Son. They hear his voice. They respond to the truth. They love the Christ. They do the works of Abraham, which is to say, the work of faith. The children or slaves of Satan likewise respond to him. They do his work despite declarations to the contrary. They resist the truth. They cannot hear the Word. They lie, kill, lust, hate, and are bloated with pride.

Now the real temptation, as we read today's text, is to reflect on this contrast and disapprovingly shake our heads at the Jewish leaders. After all, they were professing to be Abraham's seed while plotting to kill the Son of God! However, we must instead turn the spotlight on us. As justice people, we can sometimes find ourselves in both camps. We recognize the Son. We hear his voice and respond to the call by doing good works. We love the Christ. But sometimes we also resist the truth and cannot hear the Word. We lie. We lust, hate, and despair, and we can often be puffed up with pride. While working each day to tear down systemic oppression, we can still, through sin, make ourselves into slaves. Despite our lives and good deeds, we find we must examine our own hearts again and again so that we may cast off, lay aside, and break free from every weight.

But this is not an indictment to jump on the hamster wheel of trying—trying to do better or striving to do more. Trying to work harder or longer. Trying to stop this or start that. No, rather it is an invitation to examine our hearts and acknowledge where we may have resisted God's truth or failed to believe.

In John 8:32, Jesus said, "You shall know the truth, and the truth shall make you free." Free from the tyranny of our flesh to reside in the liberty of the spirit. Free from the goal of pleasing God to the joy of knowing God. As we obey the teachings of Christ, we come to know the truth, and that truth leads us from being slaves to the freedom of being sons and daughters.

PART 4

THE MESSAGE: GOOD NEWS

"PASSOVER SONG"

SUNG BY URBAN DOXOLOGY

21

FORGIVE US OUR DEBTS

In Him we have redemption through His blood, the
forgiveness of sins, according to the riches of His grace.

Ephesians 1:7

READING: LUKE 17:1-5

Some time ago I was out with a friend whose negative behavior
surprised me. It left me in a strange, uncomfortable place. I
struggled to find a word for the emotion I was feeling—the dull,
sober nothingness that had slowly crept over my heart toward him.
When it persisted the next day, I chose to wrestle with it rather than
ignore it.

Craig is a fellow comrade in arms, another Jesus follower committed to kingdom living and loving, and a pursuer of God, truth, and
justice. But last night, Craig was less *than I had made him to be* and
today I felt . . . disappointed.

So this morning I asked God what I should do with that. He began
by acknowledging my disappointment: "Craig has sinned against
you. That's why you feel as you do."

"Yes, but what do I do with that?" I said. "How can I forgive something that hasn't been confessed or repented of?" Then I thought about Jesus, dying for my sins—past, present, and future. (Okay, I walked right into that.)

But the truth is that the Father has forgiven me for things I haven't confessed or repented, and for things I haven't even done yet. When I get around to doing them, while confession is desired, he has forgiven me whether I own up to it or not. Forgiveness, he reminds me, is not about letting things go. Forgiveness is choosing to apply the price that has already been paid—the blood of Jesus—to the charge on the offender's account. Yes, my friend was found guilty, but the sentence for his crime, like my own, has already been executed against Christ. And the Father has found that sacrifice sufficient.

My anger and resentment are more about me wanting to exact my own form of punishment and, perhaps, my lack of faith in God's justice. Jesus said offenses are sure to come. We can count on that. Our ability to respond appropriately to the offense is a matter of faith. In this instance, I had not told my friend that he offended me. I chose rather to walk around with that resentment in my heart. I sinned against him while being angry that he had sinned against me! My dishonest heart did not provide the opportunity for his repentance. In my time of reflection I realized that there was a part of me that did not want him to repent because then I would have to release him from the prison I created for him by my own self-righteous judgement.

Sometimes in these instances we want to yell, "But what about what he did?" And God responds, "Yes, I know, but what about what I did?" Then he holds out the nail-scarred hands to show us. I stubbornly ball up my fists and momentarily walk away, not yet quite willing to concede. I think of Jonah and the cost of his resistance, and I wonder if my position is worth a possible three-day stint in the damp, dark belly of my pride.

When people offend us, it is understandable to be angry or hurt and to desire an apology. When we offend others, it is good and beneficial to acknowledge that and offer one. And when our sins are also considered crimes, there may be criminal prosecution, conviction, and consequence. But in any case, our forgiveness of ourselves or others is not optional. To withhold it is to reject the perfect sacrifice of Jesus Christ for sin.

So I choose to release my friend Craig. I will not seek to shame him or make him pay for his crime.

> "Vengeance *is* Mine, I will repay," says the Lord.
>
> ROMANS 12:19

And with that decision, that loosing and letting go, I feel the numbness in my heart begin to fade. Jesus says,

"If he sins against you seven times in a day, and seven times in a day returns to you, saying, 'I repent,' you shall forgive him." And the apostles said to the Lord, "Increase our faith." (Luke 17:4-5)

22

IN THE BEGINNING

But He *was* wounded for our transgressions,
He *was* bruised for our iniquities;
The chastisement for our peace *was* upon Him,
And by His stripes we are healed.

Isaiah 53:5

READING: ISAIAH 53

A holy God created a perfect man, placed him in the perfect environment, and provided him with intimate relationship and endless resources. Then that man disrupted it all in one foolish act of disobedience that brought suffering and death to all of mankind.

However, God, still desiring to have an intimate relationship with man, initiates a plan for restoration. Since God is just, sin must receive its promised wage. He cannot look the other way or "let it go," for this would destroy the balance of the universe, and God would cease to be God. No, sin must ultimately lead to death. Yet, God has also provided that the death of the sinless shall as certainly lead to life.

I was nobody special—a black girl raised in a two-bedroom row house in a poor neighborhood in southwest Philly. My parents didn't graduate from college or even finish high school. And no one rich or famous knew my name. Still, God decided to save me from the slow death that was my life. He reordered my steps. He rewrote my story. I don't have a dramatic tale. I wasn't strong or brave enough to get into much trouble. I was just a child born with a terminal illness called sin in a nation corrupted by the same.

The good news is that Jesus offers us not only a substitutionary death but also a substitutionary life. My sin was cancelled out by his perfection. His torturous death produced vibrant life in me. Born in sin, I began dying from inception. Now born again, I am becoming more and more alive. As they bound him, God loosed me. As they nailed him, God freed me. As he was broken, I was made whole.

Carrying this amazingly good news within us, we are charged by Christ to move throughout our small part of the world to share it. Despite our sin and transgressions, we have been made right with the God of justice. All accounts have been reconciled. The wayward child can return home.

> The chastisement for our peace *was* upon Him,
> And by His stripes we are healed.
>
> ISAIAH 53:5

But just as surely as our word and ministry is one of reconciliation, our work is a work of justice. Attempting to live this righteous life in an unrighteous society or system is like trying to walk a straight line across a slanted floor on the warped deck of a small ship in a storm.

Christ suffered and sacrificed, not just to save us from sin but to also deliver us to the peace of God. This peace, *shalom* in Hebrew, was purchased with his stripes. It's more than the absence of conflict with the Father; it is also the inclusion of the wholeness, completeness, soundness, health, safety, and prosperity that Jesus bled and died to give us. Sharing the good news then includes fixing the slanted floor, working to right the ship, and at times raising our voices to speak to the storm.

This justice work is the effort to realign behaviors and treatments, and procedures and policies, to that which is right or fair. The plumb line of fairness is the one that was set at the beginning by a Holy God in his perfect world, one in which each living soul had intimate relationship and sufficient resource. Every degree of deviation from that line is an effort by some to reestablish the status quo and tip the scales toward injustice.

The Spirit of God, from the beginning to now, groans within these newly born hearts for the peace of justice. In response we must lift our voices and raise our hands. Quench not the Spirit.

23

SIGNS AND WONDERS

Behold, I lay in Zion
A chief cornerstone, elect, precious,
And he who believes on Him will by no means be put to shame.

1 Peter 2:6

READING: I PETER 2:1-10

It always irks me a little when people say that they must get out to a mountain or the woods to have some time with God. I'm a city girl through and through. While some of my friends coo and gush over hiking paths and bike trails and make weekend plans for camping and fishing, my pulse quickens when I see a city skyline at dusk. My best vacations involve discovering new sights, sounds, and smells in old cities and towns around the world.

Still, while I may not get enthused about the thought of sitting on a lake, holding a pole, I have never been more mindful of God's glory than the first time I stood, eyes filled with tears, on the ridge of the Grand Canyon. I have never been more aware of his power than when standing on a platform that vibrated with the thunder of the roaring waters of Niagara Falls. And I have never been more conscious of God's presence than when hearing his whisper as I stared into the darkness of night by the quiet waters of Key West. Mountains, waterfalls, and vast canyons are the monuments that point us to the Creator.

Cities, I must concede, are monuments that largely point to the creativity and achievement of humanity. Highways and bridges, museums and malls, and manicured parks and looming skyscrapers are all affixed with plaques and cornerstones to honor the accomplishments of men and women (though usually men). Historically, it was the city cathedral that pointed to the majesty of God. Beautiful structures with stories inscribed in stained glass windows; carvings in cedar, marble, and stone; and lofty ceilings arching upward, along with crosses and steeples, point the eye and mind to the Savior.

But today, many church buildings have been closed, and the old, stately cathedrals are being converted into *(cringe)* theaters and loft apartments. As our cities swell with a return flight of people where schools, coffee shops, and even bars have become the new worship centers, where will the visible markers be that remind us of the power and presence of God?

> You also, as living stones, are being built up a spiritual house, a holy priesthood, to offer up spiritual sacrifices acceptable to God through Jesus Christ.
>
> 1 PETER 2:5

In the design of the Father, we are God's building, each of us a brick. Together, like a steeple, we point above the noise to the all-knowing and powerful God who is still extending his hand toward us, inviting us into new life. Daily, we are called to offer the sacrifice of time, resources, and space for our neighbors and friends. Our redemption stories create the design in the stained-glass windows. Our testimonies are in the carvings of its walls. We are the place of refuge and sanctuary within each community. Our mouths become God's pulpit, our ears his confessional, and our arms holy ground.

It would be easier to point people toward a beautiful monument or send them into a building. In buildings, you can distinguish the sacred from the common with flickering candles and red velvet ropes. You can prevent bad impressions with business hours and locked doors and limit access when things are untidy. But living cathedrals sometimes get messy right at the moment when people stop by. We may yell at our kids in the market, honk our horns at the strangers driving beside us, or ignore a call we should take. Our lives are unworthy to be displayed on the ceiling of any chapel, and yet we are the signposts that have been chosen—the tabernacle where God meets humanity.

> But we have this *precious* treasure [the good news about salvation] in [unworthy] earthen vessels [of human frailty], so that the grandeur *and* surpassing greatness of the power will be [shown to be] from God [His sufficiency] and not from ourselves.
>
> 2 CORINTHIANS 4:7 (AMP)

Speaking of Jesus' incarnation, John writes, "And the Word became flesh and dwelt among us, and we beheld His glory, the glory as of the only begotten of the Father, full of grace and truth"

(John 1:14). Today, the incarnation is still evident—church buildings are replaced with a church body—and in us, as we yield, the glory of the Lord is revealed . . . in the city.

24

TAKEOVER

"I have told you these things, so that in Me you may have
[perfect] peace. In the world you have tribulation *and*
distress *and* suffering, but be courageous [be confident, be
undaunted, be filled with joy]; I have overcome the world."
[My conquest is accomplished, My victory abiding.]

John 16:33 (AMP)

READING: JOHN 16:28-33

Our understanding of justice has been shaped by the world we live in. In our world, justice is a complex system created to govern how we act and interact, keep order, and punish those who cross the ever-moving lines. In our nation, we like to say that justice is blind, but many of us have caught sight of her peeking from under that blindfold and tipping the scales to favor particular groups or positions. In our nation, justice looks a lot like revenge or retribution meted out with prejudice to calm fears or satisfy the anger or pain of loss.

But God's justice is different. Biblical references to the word *justice* mean "to make right." It is a relational term. So, the work of justice involves bringing people back into right relationship with God, one another, and creation. It is rooted in his divine nature and always working to realign us with his divine will. Injustice distorts, disfigures, or destroys these relationships. When I step back and look at the world with its corruption, greed, and hatefulness, I wonder how we will ever get to God's justice here.

The world (*kosmos* in Greek), with all its diverse languages and colors and landscapes, is still but one system. And that system, according to biblical scholars, is ethically bad. The word *world* in the Bible refers to the order or arrangement of unbelieving humankind organized by Satan himself. It is based on cosmic principles of force, greed, selfishness, ambition, and pleasure. Its power is military might. So, though it may be outwardly religious, scientific, cultured, and elegant, it is upheld by armed force and dominated by satanic principles.

Jesus says, "I have overcome the world" (John 16:33). Not, I *will* overcome it. Not, I'm *going to* overcome it some day in the sweet by and by. No, I *have* overcome it. Past tense, over and done. Check it off the list. World overcome.

> You are of God, little children, and have
> overcome them, because He who is in you
> is greater than he who is in the world.
>
> 1 JOHN 4:4

It's like Jesus and the enemy are involved in a high-stakes chess game, and Jesus, in what looks like the middle of the game, knocks over the opponent's king, gets up from the table, and calls "checkmate" over his shoulder as he strolls away. And we, in confusion, hang around the chessboard. We walk through the next six to eight moves with furrowed brows, whispering to each other. Then some time later, we step back, mouths open in disbelief, as we finally arrive at the conclusion that Jesus announced an hour before: checkmate.

We, who get to the end of our days with our hands dirty, grubby faced, sweaty, and panting from our struggles with anyone from clueless neighbors to city hall, then wonder how can this be?

I was no business major, okay, but I understand that every now and then in the world of commerce, a hostile takeover occurs when one company (the target) is purchased by another. If the management of the target company doesn't agree with the takeover, the acquiring company accomplishes the takeover by going directly to the target company's shareholders (owners) or fighting to replace management. If the owners agree, the deal is done. Now management may, for a time, keep showing up for work, coming up with tricks and schemes to try to hold on to things as they were. They may huff and puff and bluster with the insistence that they are still in charge, ordering everyone around who doesn't know any better. But the fact remains that they are finished, and it's only a matter of time before the new management team is put in place and the name on the building is changed.

Jesus came into the world to execute a hostile takeover, to reset the justice system. Satan was not in agreement, but he was not the owner, and so it happened without his consent. Our hearts are now free to choose to live under the rule of a loving God. Still, there is a whole evil cosmic system in place, blustering through religion and science and culture, upheld by military force, fighting desperately to preserve the appearance that the old management is still in charge. But Jesus reassures us today with words of comfort. Wipe your face and wash your hands and be of good cheer. The deal is done. The price has been paid. Father and Son shook hands, and the new building sign is on the way. Choose a desk and set out your pictures. I have overcome the world.

25

THE EMMAUS ROAD

> Then He said to them, "O foolish ones, and slow of heart to
> believe in all that the prophets have spoken! Ought not the Christ
> to have suffered these things and to enter into His glory?"

Luke 24:25-26

READING: LUKE 24:13-34

The road to Emmaus is a familiar one. It is the path we take every day. It is the road we travel as we go about our daily lives, heading to work or school, to visit loved ones or run errands. It is the path of life. And as we go, like the disciples in the text, we often wonder and discuss, we debate and muse, we complain and moan about the events of our day and the hopes that have been built or dashed by them.

Sometimes things don't turn out as we thought they would, and we are perplexed. The promises of God appear unfulfilled, and we are frustrated or angry or at a loss as to what he is doing and why. Occasionally, we meet up with friends or strangers along that road who, like us, are weary, disillusioned, and ready to give up on the belief that things will ever change or on the possibility that God even cares.

> And it came to pass, that, while they
> communed together and reasoned, Jesus
> himself drew near, and went with them.
>
> LUKE 24:15 (KJV)

It is often while we are rehearsing our issues or scratching our heads in agitation that Jesus himself appears. As we're listening to our neighbor, or the man next to us on the plane, or as we ourselves are venting about the economy or the election or the kids, Jesus shows up unannounced and unnoticed until he raises a question within our hearts. "What are you talking about?" he says. "Why are you sad, anxious, or upset?" Then, unaware of who it is that has whispered the question, we start in on the who, what, and why. God listens intently, waiting for us to take a breath, and when he speaks our hearts begin to burn within us.

Jesus appears to the two disciples as they go along their journey. He listens and challenges them on what they should know and understand. He teaches them. He abides with them. He serves them. And through these acts they come to know him and believe.

I am often like those disciples when things don't go as I imagine they would. When God fails to follow my plans, I also find myself muttering my complaints aloud and lumbering down the road in frustration. I rehearse the events, whining or complaining to friends, or shaking my head in disappointment. I forget what he told me. I forget where I've been and all that I've known to be true until he interrupts my laments with his Word. When I quiet my heart to listen for his voice, and when I approach the table to receive and acknowledge his blessings, my eyes are opened. I recognize the hand and face of God.

We don't know why the disciples were headed to the village of Emmaus. They may have been on their way home. However, sometimes when we are disappointed or confused, we can get off track, moving away from God's will or plan to go down paths of our own choosing. We may be headed back to former people, places, or things to lick our wounds in the comfort of the familiar. Thankfully, Jesus shows up on our back roads to remind us of what he told us and where we've been. In our time with him, we not only see who he is but also can remember who we are and where we need to be.

Then, like the disciples, we often realize that God has been with us all along. Despite how it looks, we have not been left victim to our circumstances or abandoned to a situation. Rather, Jesus is risen. He is still God, and things are indeed moving along according to plan—his plan. So, finding this joy, we gather our courage and return to share this news again with others. Regardless of the weather, the White House, our finances, family, or foes, Christ is risen indeed, and in this we will rejoice.

26

WORD MADE FLESH

Receive with meekness the implanted word,

which is able to save your souls.

James 1:21

READING: JAMES 1:13-27

The challenge of our lives as believers is that no matter how significant our cause or work may be, we know that as followers of Jesus, it is not enough to *say* the right thing. We must also *believe* it. It is not sufficient to do good. We must incarnate good and be the goodness in our sphere of influence.

If you're like me, there are days when you think, *Why do I have to do it the "right" way? Why can't I yell and cuss and fight like everybody else when people do me wrong? Why can't I cut corners or fudge a bit on the numbers? Why can't I just quit and walk away because I'm tired or hurt or scared? After all,* we say, *even Jesus turned over some tables, right?* But Jesus wasn't having a tantrum. He wasn't going off on the moneychangers because they got on his last nerve. We may imagine it that way because that's how we've interpreted the pictures in our children's Bible, or because it makes us feel better to think that Jesus was having a bad day and had it "up to here" with those jokers, which we then want to interpret as giving us permission by example to do the same. Perhaps we could if we were just living our natural lives. You know, the lives we were originally born into, the wretches we were before receiving this amazing grace. If only we could un-sing the songs and unbelieve the truth, then we could go back to our small, dark, broken lives and live as we darn well please.

But we can't. Not if we believe that stuff about Jesus dying for us.

> For the love of Christ constraineth us; because we thus judge, that if one died for all, then were all dead:
>
> And that he died for all, that they which live should not henceforth live unto themselves, but unto him which died for them, and rose again.
>
> 2 CORINTHIANS 5:14-15 (KJV)

No, if Jesus died for me, in my place, as if he were me, then by receiving this salvation gift I have agreed to live for him, in his place, as if I were him—not just doing things he would do (WWJD) but the way he would do them—living the life he would live.

Of course, attempting to do this in my own strength is impossible. Every ounce of this flesh wants to rise up a hundred times a day against the racist and the sexist, against the politicians and the historians, against the assumptions and the omissions. But Jesus is more than a God above us. He is God within us. He is the Word implanted in us in the person of the Holy Spirit, living within the heart of believers. We too become Word made flesh. We are transformed, moved from death to life, living epistles read by all.

So, the *how* is just as important as the *what*. To pull off the *how*, we must engage the Spirit. To give in to his *how*, the flesh must die again and again. To live in not just the *what* and the *why* but also the *how* of Christ requires a trust in the wisdom, faithfulness, and goodness of God and his specific concern for us. It requires a trust that he will avenge us and protect us, that he has a plan that is working for us, and that his plan is for good.

God is up to something that is bigger than this moment. When we interact in our homes and communities, speak our words, and handle our business, then family, neighbors, friends, and strangers should know that they have been in the presence of God. The word implanted in us *will* produce fruit. A life without fruit is a life unchanged, a heart uninhabited. True salvation and transformation results in a true religion—a changed interaction with the world (widows, orphans, and the like) and ourselves.

Religion is often defined as a collection of beliefs organized into a system. Pure religion, however, moves from beliefs, systems, and views into action and impact. Word made flesh.

27

PRIVILEGE

The voice of one crying in the wilderness:
"Prepare the way of the LORD;
Make straight in the desert
A highway for our God."

Isaiah 40:3

READING: ISAIAH 40:1-5

We live in a society that accepts different shades but not different colors, allows different ethnicity but resists different culture. It sends the message that different clothes, hair, and skin tones are not only okay but even worthy of imitation as long as you think the way we think, use the language we use, and do things the way we do them. After all, the words we use are "proper" English. The way we think only makes good sense, and the way we do it is the most appropriate, after all.

"Well, all people think that way," they argue. "Everyone assumes their way is the best way and right way." Perhaps there is some truth to that, but not everyone has the power and resources to make their personal values and preferences the law and policy.

Figure 1. Equality versus Equity

We look at the popular cartoon image of the children attempting to watch the ball game over the fence and can acknowledge the obvious advantage of the tall child over the others. However, this acknowledgement does not unmask the unspoken, perhaps unconscious belief that the tall child somehow deserves to have that view in a way that the others do not. He has earned that place of privilege, and any efforts to level the playing field would rob him of what is rightfully due, or it would unjustly reward the others with something they do not deserve.

So even though the tall one consciously and publicly agrees with the redistribution of resources or position, he will often continuously, though perhaps unconsciously, look for opportunities to either reduce these adjustments or increase the requirements to receive them.

However, Jesus comes in the power and authority of heaven and all the privilege born to him as a healthy, professional, Jewish male— and he chooses another way. In his ministry and lifestyle, both public and private, he humanizes and honors those most maligned and neglected by the masses by treating them as equals. He does this without regard for their prior activities or lineage. There are no inquiries about work history, money management, or reckless lifestyles. He simply responds to each one as one made in the image of God. And where inequities have put them at an unfair disadvantage, he challenges or removes them by providing food to the hungry; health to the lame; regard for children; and respect, care, and even friendship for women and Gentiles.

He invited himself to dine with a tax collector and let a woman wash his feet with her hair. He made time and space for children, touched lepers, and walked through towns others chose to walk around. By so doing, the overlooked were no longer invisible. The ones previously left out were now included, heard, and seen.

Jesus didn't just preach and teach a justice message. He lived a life that demonstrated it. In like manner, our message of love and justice must move beyond our activist activities and spill over into our active lives on a daily basis. It is in the way we conduct business and who with, which events we choose to attend and who we invite to ours. It's what we choose to promote and celebrate, where we shop and take our children, what we read or listen to or watch. It's in the voices we choose to amplify and the people we invite or bring to the table. And sometimes it's how or for whom we willingly choose to give up our seat. In these simple lifestyle choices that we make every day, we fulfill the words of the prophet. We exalt the valleys and lower the mountains, make the rough places smooth, and make the crooked straight. And sometimes, for the glory of the Lord, we even tear down the stupid fence.

> Every valley shall be exalted
> And every mountain and hill brought low;
> The crooked places shall be made straight
> And the rough places smooth;
> The glory of the LORD shall be revealed,
> And all flesh shall see *it* together;
> For the mouth of the LORD has spoken.
>
> ISAIAH 40:4-5

PART 5

THE METHOD: LOVE

"FIGHTS FOR ME"

SUNG BY URBAN DOXOLOGY

28

THE MANDATE TO LOVE

And this is His commandment: that we should believe
on the name of His Son Jesus Christ and love one
another, as He gave us commandment.

I John 3:23

READING: I JOHN 3:16-24

Love is an overly familiar word whose concept ever eludes us. Often confused with *lust, need, jealousy,* or *pain,* love is a most familiar mystery.

I remember the first time I attached the word to a feeling I had for a boy. Someone had injured his fragile feelings, and he had shared his pain with me. Immediately I too felt injured and then enraged. I wanted to hurt the person who had hurt him, to lash out in his defense. When I was able to step back from my feelings and examine them, I was surprised at the intensity of my emotion toward someone I did not know and who had done nothing directly to me. In that moment, I named that emotion: *love. I love him,* I thought with simultaneous terror and joy. *I love him.*

But love is more than a feeling or sudden flash of emotion, and it's bigger than teenage angst or joy. It demands more from us than poetic words and romantic gestures. It summons everything and requires all. It is infinite and therefore challenges our finite understanding.

> **By this we know love, because He laid down His life for us.**
>
> 1 JOHN 3:16

So heaven commanded an enormous, simple, sacrificial act. This is what makes it possible to understand, what brings it within our grasp, what makes it tangible. Love became a person, stepping into our pain and walking in our grief. Love willingly, voluntarily died, and in so doing made new life available to you and me.

> **And we also ought to lay down *our* lives for the brethren.**
>
> 1 JOHN 3:16

What does it mean to lay down my life today? A fiery post or a clever tweet? The purchase of a new pair of Toms (for ourselves) or a generous check? Is love captured in a move from a suburban mainline church to an in-town, non-denominational church plant? If God wants to use my life to define the word, what on earth does *love* mean?

As with Christ, in you and me, by the Spirit of God, love is transformed from a romantic notion into a human being. Love becomes a hug on a hard day. Love gives up a Friday night to watch a neighbor's kids. Love sits beside me in the hospital waiting room, stands with me at the graveside of my mother, and walks with me in a protest rally in the street. And at God's command, love dies. This obedience does not destroy but rather emboldens us.

> But whosoever has this world's goods, and sees
> his brother in need, and shuts up his heart from
> him, how does the love of God abide in him?
>
> 1 JOHN 3:17

To turn our backs on the hungry requires us to squelch the prompting of the Spirit of God within us. To become comfortable with the cruelty of racism necessitates that I close my eyes to another's humanity as well as my own. In order to deny a cup of water to a thirsty child while hoarding a stream, I must block out the image of God in his face and mar the same on my own.

> My little children, let us not love in word
> or in tongue, but in deed and in truth.
>
> 1 JOHN 3:18

Love does not come in little, velvet boxes. It does not bruise or misuse our bodies or demand we sell our souls. While often intangible, it is almost always visible through sacrifice, compassion, and generosity. Love is how we know or recognize God in our work and deeds. It is our motivation and result. It never fails.

29

CLARITY

Because the foolishness of God is wiser than men, and
the weakness of God is stronger than men.

I Corinthians 1:25

READING: I CORINTHIANS 1:25-31

When I think of all the hard things, all the mean and downright evil
things that have been done to God's children who live in black bodies,
an angry sorrow wells up in my heart and spills over into tears. The
fact that we have survived is nothing short of miraculous. It seems
that God has chosen us, like Israel, to be a people who he dwells with
to reveal his power and sovereignty throughout the earth. Within us,
in the very cells of our being, is a reed that cannot be broken, a light
that will not be snuffed out.

Even in the midst of such hate, we live.

Honestly, my heart beats a little faster with anxious fear when I
see a menacing gun rack and oversized flag on the backs of giant
pickup trucks. The trucks always seem to be following a little too
closely, driven by men in dark shades wearing red, weathered

baseball caps. Men, I imagine, who take pleasure in dangling nooses from the trees of college campuses or marching with tiki torches through the streets of small towns. Men, I imagine, who celebrate the passing of crushing, dehumanizing policies meant to intimidate, humiliate, and separate a people made in the image of God.

> But God has chosen the foolish things of the world to put to shame the wise, and God has chosen the weak things of the world to put to shame the things which are mighty; and the base things of the world and the things which are despised God has chosen, and the things which are not, to bring to nothing the things that are.
>
> I CORINTHIANS 1:27-28

Perhaps they marvel, like me, at the miraculous reality that we are still here. How can it be, except that the Lord our God is with us? We are upheld by the power of the Almighty. Our strength, talent, and tenacity continue to confound, lying always just beyond reach, just outside the enemy's control. Evil's colorful trappings, numerous academic letters, and lofty towers appear weak, small, and impotent next to us. So, they come with chains and whips, the swinging noose and prison bars, to steal the children, withhold the land, break the promises, and squash the dreams with evil science, distorted history, plots, schemes, and endless lies. Despite it all, or perhaps because of it, we rise and grow and adapt and thrive.

They do not understand us, cannot contain us, and will not control us or limit our capacity. We are the rose that grows out of concrete, the fire that flickers, smolders, smokes, and then reignites. Why?

Because God has placed within us that portion of himself that is eternal, and the hope of all that is living is coursing through our veins. Not because we are more important or special—but simply because he has willed it so.

Fear subsides and hatred, fear's ugly cousin, is kept at bay as I think about these things. No weapon formed against us shall prosper, and every tongue that rises in judgement shall be condemned. The world indeed is presently a hard place. Perhaps for some of us it has always been. But it doesn't have to harden us. We are sent by our Savior as sheep among wolves, but we are not wolves. Wise as serpents, harmless as doves, we are the sheep of his pasture, the things that are not bringing to nothing the things that are, so that he might be glorified.

Ironically, despite everything hate has done or will ever do, if a hand is extended in peace or contrition, we are compelled to receive it. And what they so long desired to take, in the strength of divine love, we would share. Because that is who *we* are. We are his.

30

LOVE THAT COVERS A MULTITUDE

Then David lamented with this lamentation
over Saul and over Jonathan his son.

2 Samuel 1:17

READING: 2 SAMUEL 1:17-27

The bond hearing in North Charleston, South Carolina, was the first
public appearance of Dylann Roof, the twenty-one-year-old who shot
and killed nine people at a prayer meeting in a historic African
American church. When the judge invited relatives of the victims to
make statements, one by one, while acknowledging their pain, those
who chose to speak also offered words of forgiveness and prayers
that the accused would receive the mercy of God. And the kingdom
of darkness was shaken.

Eight years prior, the watching world was stunned and inspired
as an Amish community, still grieving the loss of their children in a
school shooting, offered not only words of forgiveness but also attended the burial of the killer and hugged his wife and other family

members. A year later, following several other deliberate acts of forgiveness, these parents and members of their community donated money to the widow and children of the man who killed their children.

Years later, when I read these stories, I am still moved to tears at the enormity of their love and obedience to Christ.

In the same way, I marvel at how loving and respectful David could be of Saul. Fueled by jealousy and fear, Saul pursued him for years and sought to take his life. David was forced to live on the run, even hiding for a time in a foreign land. But regardless of how long or how often Saul threatened him, when presented with the opportunity to retaliate, David resisted and showed more mercy and compassion for his enemy than many of us have for our friends.

> ### And forgive us our trespasses, as we forgive those who trespass against us.
>
> THE LORD'S PRAYER, BASED ON MATTHEW 6:12

I think about David and the Amish and the Charlotte church families and must conclude that this clemency, this level of forgiveness, is unnatural. It moves beyond what is expected or required. It is available only by God's grace—the power to do what we ought to accomplish his will. When we yield to that grace, to that power of the Spirit, we make God visible on the earth.

I think my attempts at forgiveness most often fall far below this ideal. I let it go today only to have it resurface tomorrow. Or I pardon you right now but keep you at arm's length moving forward, ensuring you never again enjoy the privilege of my full trust. My carnal forgiveness is no more than that the world offers without the Christ.

But to forgive as I have been forgiven, to let go of my right to be right and to remind you of your wrongs, requires something more. Something higher and more excellent. Radical kingdom forgiveness, ultimately, is an act of faith. It is an active, deliberate decision we make, despite the severity of the offense, to release the offender and a commitment to look for a tangible way or ways to demonstrate that pardon. It is also the choice to release ourselves from the bitter, destructive entanglement that results from holding another person captive. It is hard, and it is painful, and it is impossible to do authentically in the flesh.

David named Saul as God's anointed despite all that Saul had done.

> The Lord forbid that I should stretch out my hand against the Lord's anointed.
>
> 1 SAMUEL 26:11

When I see my enemy as one made in the image of God, or as God's child, it allows me to choose to have compassion on him. Peter cuts off the ear of the soldier who came to arrest Jesus, and Jesus puts it back on, healing the soldier. Jesus prays for forgiveness for his executioners while they are torturing him. He restores fellowship with the disciple that betrayed him not once but three times. His relationship to the Father and the Father's love and relationship to his enemies outweigh their actions toward him. He entrusts his life and the lives of his enemies to the righteous judgement of his Father. Oh, that I may love God like that!

Let your love, O Lord, surpass my hate. Then I would do my brother no harm because of what he means to you. This allows me to love the racist like Martin Luther King and Mahatma Gandhi and John M. Perkins did. This allows us to see their brokenness and mourn their loss. My love for God must cause me to relinquish my hatred of others. This is the love that conquers all. This is the power that changes the world.

31

SALVATION IS COME

God was in Christ, reconciling the world unto himself,
not imputing their trespasses unto them; and hath
committed unto us the word of reconciliation.

2 Corinthians 5:19 (KJV)

READING: LUKE 19:1-10

In the modern age of the selfie, we delight in capturing pictures of ourselves with friends or family at various places or events. Better still is the opportunity to post a Facebook, Instagram, or Snapchat photo or video of ourselves with a famous singer, actor, author, athlete, or political figure. We want to shout out our connections with the rich or famous, perhaps secretly hoping to increase our own prestige by association.

But Jesus goes out of his way to associate himself with the least of these: thieves, prostitutes, and despised tax collectors. Zacchaeus was honored that Jesus even acknowledged him. Still, Jesus went further, calling him by name and announcing a visit to his house.

Jesus made a public connection between himself and Zacchaeus, who was an outcast, a sinner, a sellout Jew.

We hear Jesus yell to him over the noise of the crowds, "Hey, Zach! Yo, buddy, come here, let me holla at you. I want to hang out at your place tonight." Can you imagine the buzz that swept through that crowd, the raised eyebrows, the gaping mouths, the whispers behind cupped palms? "Jesus is talking to that guy! He acts like he knows him. What?! He's going to his house! Doesn't he know who he is?"

Zacchaeus's home is the house we miss . . . intentionally. He's the one we glare at with crossed arms and pursed lips when he passes by us on the street. He's the one we blame for all our troubles, the one we are sent to rescue people from. We don't go to his house. He's one of them, the problem.

Yet despite the fine clothes and the big house, the gold jewelry and the lavish lifestyle, Zacchaeus was up a tree, literally. He was lost. He had left his people and his God to pursue the power and prestige of wealth, and as a result, the people he rejected had rejected him. However, Jesus, choosing to stay on mission, pursues him. Jesus remembers what we often forget—sometimes what looks like "success" is actually "lost" with better clothes.

Seen and publicly acknowledged by Jesus, Zacchaeus quickly comes down from his perch and receives the Christ, calling him Lord, not Rabbi like the Pharisees did. Still, trapped by his religious upbringing, he tries to make himself right by following the rules, fulfilling the law, and promising to restore what was taken with interest. Perhaps that would have been enough to satisfy the naysayers who watched the scene, gawking and saying, "Hey, that sounds like a win-win for everybody, ain't that right, Jesus?" However, Jesus lets them all know that salvation cannot be earned by money or good deeds, but instead salvation is offered when we come to him, as it's offered to all of us, by grace through faith, not because we are deserving but because God is good.

> ### For the Son of man is come to seek and to save that which was lost.
>
> LUKE 19:10 (KJV)

Years ago, I had a mentor named Greg who made it his mission to teach what it means to see and live in the kingdom of God. One of the many ways he did that was by taking a group of us to visit a prison and youth detention center. The first several times we went, my friends and I just sat quietly in the prison chapel and listened as Greg talked and shared Scriptures with the men, women, and youth who were detained there. However, on one occasion Greg asked me to be prepared to teach the women. I was in my early twenties and terrified. I was an honor-roll student who grew up in the church. (It never occurred to me that perhaps they were too.) I had led inside a church building before, but I just kept thinking, *What do I have to say to these young women who are behind bars?*

A few nights before we went to the prison, I stood staring out my kitchen window and asked God that very question: "Lord, I don't have an exciting testimony to share. What could they possibly care to hear from me? We have nothing in common. What do I say?" And then, through the words of a familiar hymn, God reminded me: "I once was lost but now I'm found. Was blind but now I see." We were not that different after all.

Zacchaeus' life was changed because he was curious enough, diligent enough, and desperate enough to climb a tree for the possibility of a glimpse of the Christ. Have we said enough, cared enough, or loved enough to create that kind of curiosity? In our zeal to address a cause, have we dismissed or despised a people? Jesus looks at Zacchaeus through the leaves of his wealth and his politics and responds. In so doing, he reminds the crowd and us that the oppressor too is made in the image of God and is included in his plan of redemption. Jesus came to seek and save that which was lost, and our God rewards those who climb trees to diligently seek him.

THE WAY AND CHARACTER OF THE RIGHTEOUS

The steps of a *good* man are ordered by the
LORD, and He delights in his way.

Psalm 37:23

READING: PSALM 37:21-31

One of the challenges of pursuing kingdom justice is that you must do it without compromising godly character. If I make eloquent speeches or write passionate blogs without love, it's just noise. If I am gifted with a prophetic message, if I'm deeply wise, brilliant, or fearless but fail at loving, I am nothing. And if I deny myself my North American, middle-class comforts to feed the poor or relocate to an under-resourced neighborhood but do not embody the attitude, humility, and nature of divine love, my sacrifice is worthless. As a believer, I am challenged every day to fight evil without becoming it.

I must remind myself that the character of righteousness is merciful, generous, and good. It's the result of understanding that we have been gifted with grace, blessed with an inheritance, and promised a future. However, I also remember that this promise does not exempt us from challenges or difficulties. Nor does it make us martyrs. We are simply children straining to respond to a loving Father by loving others.

To say that our steps are "ordered" means that they are arranged or organized according to specific principles or precepts. Yet, even though our way is laid out by the Lord, we may still stumble. We sometimes give up too soon. We say the wrong thing or the right thing in the wrong way. We choose to be selfish or unforgiving, spiteful or petty. We may exaggerate the details or our role in the story. Or we quit altogether, giving in to doubts or fear or unbelief. Though I sometimes shrink in defeat when this happens, the Word of the Lord reminds me that I shall not be completely knocked out because he is walking beside me.

> Though he fall, he shall not be utterly cast down;
> For the Lord upholds *him with* His hand.
>
> PSALM 37:24

Picture it—you're shuffling along down a bumpy path, perhaps distracted or fatigued, and *whoosh*, your feet unexpectedly fly out from underneath you. Your breath catches in your throat and you brace for impact. Only it doesn't come. Instead you feel yourself suspended in the air, like a small child, your wrist held firmly by the grip of a large, strong hand until he lovingly sets you down, righted on your feet again, and you continue walking.

The ordered path is not the one he sends down alone but rather the one we walk *with* God when we give up choosing our own way.

Despite the many times we attempt to run ahead of him or get distracted by the colorful or the curious along the path, God does not abandon us. We whine or complain as our short legs grow weary, and we sometimes sink to our knees in frustrated anger. Still, we will never be orphaned or left to fend for ourselves. No, instead the invitation of the Father from Psalm 37:27 is to "Depart from evil and do good; / And dwell forevermore" with God. It is possible not only to yield but also to find delight in this way.

For many years I led a summer camp in Atlanta that included daily team-building activities. One game involved a group of about ten kids attempting to get from one side of a room to the other without touching the floor by using four or five small pillows as stepping stones. I watched as they painstakingly laid down pillows one by one, moving slowly and carefully as a unit, shifting pillows from the last position to the first again and again. At times they wobbled and leaned dangerously close to the forbidden floor, but they almost always caught or grabbed hold of one another in the nick of time.

Mr. Mike, the creator of these challenges, would sit nearby, watching with amusement as the kids inched along. Now and again, when frustrations would rise, he would call out suggestions. These were usually short, carefully worded hints meant to help them without giving too much away because the true intention of the activity was not about accomplishing the goal but rather about what they discovered about each other and themselves (and Mr. Mike) in the process.

Of course, there was always someone who would try to take a shortcut or get around a rule of the game, which would result in the entire group having to begin again. Eventually, the group would arrive on the other side together because the game is always planned with their success in mind and ordered in a way to ensure it.

Our God will not forsake us no matter how many times we fail in our trying. The security we find in that truth and his unconditional love allows us to not only speak the words of justice but also to live and serve both allies and enemies with the law of love engraved on our hearts.

33

WHO IS THAT?

They answered and said to him, "You were completely born in sins, and are you teaching us?" And they cast him out.

John 9:34

READING: JOHN 9:13-34

Every now and then, my kids and I like to watch a TV show called *Undercover Boss*. The general premise is that a corporate business owner dons a disguise and visits the ground level of their company, assuming an entry-level position alongside their employees. Over the course of several days, the disguised boss gets to see the company from the perspective of the workers, learn about their lives, and hear what they really think about their jobs and yes, even about their boss.

A few workers usually engage with the stranger, attempting to help them learn the ropes of their position, sharing tips and personal challenges along the way. At the end of the show, a few stand-out workers are called up to corporate headquarters where they discover, much to their surprise, that the bumbling temp who showed up for only a day was actually the owner of the company. At this point most of these employees are praised and rewarded for the kindness, hard work, and dedication they demonstrated to the boss. Occasionally, however, a few others are shocked and dismayed to learn that the stranger they mocked, ignored, or complained to was actually the CEO.

In Scripture, sometimes we see Jesus show up looking like an Israelite Jew and at other times like the beaten man lying by the side of the road. Some days he's the chatty, well-dressed stranger beside us in line in a crowded airport. On other days, he's the kid wearing locks and sagging pants we drive by at the bus stop, his head bobbing to the music playing through earbuds dangling from his ears. If we get stuck on the outward appearance, we can miss the gift of God standing right in front of us. If we get distracted by what we think we know or have, we can miss the wealth of what he came to give.

> Then they reviled him and said, "You are His disciple, but we are Moses' disciples."
>
> JOHN 9:28

We are sometimes the superior-minded Pharisee, whether church or nonprofit leader, as we stand before Jesus, who perhaps is disguised as an inmate, a homeless woman, or the black or brown child, asking for water. We've been doing this a while, so we know. We stand with pride in our knowledge of the Scriptures, laws, other program leaders, or "the way things are done." And Jesus, a formerly empty-handed beggar, stands before us full of the truth we need to bring new life.

We may feel uncomfortable in his gaze, exposed by his questions. But if we can will ourselves to open a conversation and adjust our posture from telling to receiving, our eyes may be opened to see the Christ. What's more, we may have the opportunity to move from the mundane to engage the miraculous and help others to do so as well.

But instead, some of us stand in trembling anger, sputtering through clenched teeth, "We're in charge here. Who are you to tell us?!" And we hate the beggar because he reminds us of the truth that we are not superior at all but rather fellow beggars, common and small. We curse him because, despite our best attempts at avoidance, he is here seeing our frailty and weakness, seemingly shouting out our failures. We do not trust his simple story or his account of transformation. We do not believe his tale of healing and new life. So, we posture and defend and send him away with angry sneers. And we reject the Lord of glory, standing in the guise of a pauper. After all, what could he possibly have to offer us?

Lord, help me not to miss you today when you're standing in front of me in unlikely vessels. Help me not to reject you because of my pride and fear. Help me rather to be open to receive from you both grace and correction and to demonstrate my gratitude by inviting others to come to you, my source of healing and new sight.

PART 6

THE REALITY: SUFFERING

"PURGE ME"

SUNG BY URBAN DOXOLOGY

34

CAST DOWN BUT
NOT DESTROYED

For we who live are always delivered to death for Jesus' sake, that
the life of Jesus also may be manifested in our mortal flesh.

2 Corinthians 4:11

READING: 2 CORINTHIANS 4:3-18

I hate being cold—absolutely hate it. It is the very definition of discomfort for me. My whole body tenses up, so much so that the muscles in my neck and shoulders ache from it afterward. So, when I asked my husband what he wanted to do for his birthday, and he replied, "Tubing!" which involves repeatedly hiking up a hill in the snow and then sliding back down on a rubber donut, it was difficult to hide my disdain: "Oh . . . wow . . . tubing. Really? Okay." I swallowed hard, breathed a long sigh, and then replied, "Sure, if that's what you want to do, let's do it." I hate the cold, but I love my husband.

As people of God, we daily find ourselves in circumstances and situations where we are asked to die—die to what we think or what we want to say, die to what we feel like doing, or even die to our impulse to remain silent or invisible. Each time we yield to this death, this crucifixion, the Christ who lives within us is made visible.

> ### So then death is working in us, but life in you.
> #### 2 CORINTHIANS 4:12

The decision to go tubing was no simple one. I wasn't prepared for hours in the snow. I had to buy a pair of boots and a water-resistant jacket, layer on clothes, drive an hour to the mountain, and pay the fees. I felt foolish, uncomfortable, and a little bit terrified. Everything within me wanted to go home. But my husband was smiling and cheering with excitement as we approached the top of the run. So I took a deep breath, climbed onto my tube, and "died."

The decision to lay down our lives for others is time-consuming and costly. Talking about justice is cheap. Living a just lifestyle is not. Empowerment is not about giving power to another. It's about giving up some of our own. Creating fairness for one group of people may mean the loss of advantage for another, or giving up space, or choosing to forgive, or leaving our warm and safe comfort zones to trudge through the snow. Every day we carry a cross. As David said, "I will not sacrifice to the LORD . . . offerings that cost me nothing" (2 Samuel 24:24 DT). Whatever the sacrifice, we trust that in our dying, as with Jesus, the Spirit will bring resurrection and that this new life will result in a praise and thanksgiving that brings yet more glory to God.

For this reason, we don't give up. We press into it. We continue to die. We climb the hill again and again.

For our light affliction, which is but for a moment, is working for us a far more exceeding *and* eternal weight of glory, while we do not look at the things which are seen, but at the things which are not seen. For the things which are seen *are* temporary, but the things which are not seen *are* eternal.

2 CORINTHIANS 4:17-18

35

OBEY YOUR THIRST

O my God, my soul is cast down within me;

therefore, I will remember You.

Psalm 42:6

READING: PSALM 42

The sun was bright and the air was cool when I set out on my walk one morning. Pandora was pumping Wide Awake Radio through my headphones, and I was feeling fine. By the time I finished my five-mile walk, my body was sending a signal that my mind translated as the word *thirst.* As I walked through my front door, I planned to make a beeline to the kitchen for a cold drink, but before I could do so, I was confronted with a problem. It was nothing major—just an annoyance from my son that had to do with wet shoes from a water balloon fight on the previous day. After addressing that matter, I got busy with other things, so it was hours before my mind returned to thoughts of water.

Sometimes that's the way we respond to the promptings of the Spirit. Distracted by the annoyances of everyday life and confronted by the constant demands of work and other responsibilities, our conversations with the Father get pushed aside, buried under the piles, or drowned out by the noise of the urgent until we are jolted by the pain of suffering.

In the throes of suffering, we are interrupted from our routines. Thirsty becomes parched, and we are left panting, like a deer, for the water of God's Spirit. Pummeled with financial concerns, rocked with health problems, or shaken by the disappointment, attack, or abandonment of the ones we love, like the psalmist we are sometimes left with a daily diet of tears. Adding insult to injury, the watching world mocks us with the taunting question, "Where is your God?"

> When I remember these *things*,
> I pour out my soul within me.
>
> PSALM 42:4

However, what disturbs us is not the accusations of the multitude but rather the resentful grumblings of our own hearts. In the midst of our suffering, we hear the questions rising from within us: *Why have you forgotten me? Have I not forsaken all and followed after you? Why are my children acting a fool? Why am I always scraping to get by? Why did our home go into foreclosure? Why is my father dying from cancer? Why is my community being wrecked by gentrification? Why is my brother still struggling with drugs? Why do I go mourning because of the oppression of the enemy? Where are you, God?!*

> The Lord will command His lovingkindness in the daytime,
> And in the night His song *shall be* with me.
>
> PSALM 42:8

When the salty waves of disappointment and disillusionment are crashing over us, we realize our dehydration and call out, though perhaps with reluctance or fear, to the only one who can save us. But the way to peace most often does not come through rescue but rather through truth and remembrance. We need not stifle the questions in our hearts. God is not put off by our anger. He also will not be shamed by our accusations. When we honestly pour out our pain before him, when we move past the polite, quiet tears to the ranting with runny noses and pounding fists, when we finally allow our heaving chest to settle down to slow, steady breaths, we begin to remember. We recall that we are not mistreated victims left abandoned or abused. God did not renege on an agreement or fail to fulfill our contract. He paid up front. While we were yet in our sin, Christ died. We, who were not a people, have been made the people of God. He has loved us without condition, forgiven our sins, and given us eternal life. He has cancelled our debt, declared us righteous, and set us free from the tyranny of sin and death. More than that, he has adopted us and called us his own. He has given us his name. When we remember the great love with which he loved us, we can begin to speak to our own souls.

> Why are you cast down, O my soul?
> And why are you disquieted within me?
> Hope in God;
> For I shall yet praise Him,
> The help of my countenance and my God.
>
> **PSALM 43:5**

On my knees, before the throne, and past my tears, I find the river of his Word and the fountain of his Spirit, and when I drink, I am refreshed to go on.

36

PRAYING TO THE WALL

Then Hezekiah turned his face toward
the wall, and prayed to the LORD.

Isaiah 38:2

READING: ISAIAH 38:1-5

We're doers: action junkies, motion sensitive, pedal-to-the-metal people. If there's a problem to be solved, an issue to be addressed, or a work to be done, we're likely to be about it. As a southern friend in Atlanta likes to say, we "get 'er done!"

We talk about issues ad nauseam, spend countless hours searching the web, and invest our miniscule expendable income buying yet another book. We meet and we march. We shout and we seethe. Then, at the end of long and frustrating days, we fall into bed exhausted. We voluntarily spend our days pushing rocks uphill. It's who we are. And every now and then, perhaps through half-open, tired eyes, we pray.

I can't count the number of times I've frantically rushed around the house, watching the clock, looking for lost keys, lost glasses, or a lost phone. Finally, in desperation, I moan out loud, "Oh, Lord, please show me. Where is it?!" Time and time again, within minutes (sometimes less), I am led directly to the pocket, pile, or closet where the lost item is waiting. And each time I wonder as I rush out the door, "Why didn't I ask you before?"

Prayer can be like the whistle on my key ring—always available but seldom used. At other times it feels like I'm yanking the string on an old lawnmower again and again until the sweat runs down my face and my back is sore, only to hear, for the twentieth time, the motor sputter and die. But attempting to address the injustices of our world without prayer is like walking away from the lawnmower and picking up a scissors.

Hezekiah, the son of King Ahaz, was twenty-five when he began to reign in Jerusalem. Hezekiah received news from the prophet Isaiah that Hezekiah's critical illness was terminal. The word from the Lord was "you will die." It was clear. It was succinct. It was definite. Hezekiah didn't respond by reviewing his will or personal effects, or drinking his way to the bottom of a bottle, or lashing out in anger at the world. No, Hezekiah turns his face to the wall and prays. Hezekiah cries out to the living God.

Prayer appears to be the exact opposite of doing. It means slowing down, standing still, taking a moment to sit in the pause, and breathe. And it is more than talking to the air or running through a list of requests. It is listening for a voice, remembering what we've known, and knowing it again. It is drawing from a well, drinking from a fountain, and having an audience with the King. When we pray, we again acknowledge that justice is not only our work but also the identity and plan of a just God being revealed in the earth. Power is released. Resources are given. Doors, windows, and hearts are opened. Minds, laws, and sometimes even the course of nature, change.

> Go and tell Hezekiah, "Thus says the LORD, the God of David your father: 'I have heard your prayer.'"
>
> ISAIAH 38:5

We're action people. Doers. But sometimes (every time) the most powerful thing we can do is turn our frustrated faces to the wall and call out to the God who made us. Acknowledging our weaknesses, fear, and total dependence on him brings us back to the divine reality that we are but children who heard a call. And in that posture we may, like Hezekiah, remind him that at the very least, we did answer.

Growing up in the thick traditions of a northern, black Baptist church, I saw, heard, and experienced prayer in many forms. I've sat, eyes closed and head bowed, alone in my room at times and in the midst of the congregation at other times. I've listened to my mother speak about a mourner's bench, and I've stood in a crowd, holding hands, at the altar. From the quiet, carefully worded, liturgical prayers of a chapel to the booming, sweat-dripping appeals from the pulpit, we pray. Not for form or fashion, ritual or show, but because we've felt, heard, seen, and known that prayer changes things, situations, and people—and sometimes, like Hezekiah, even the will of God.

Maybe you've gotten some bad news or perhaps faced some equally dire situation. Maybe for the thousandth time you've been told no, it can't be done. You can spend your days getting second, third, and fifth opinions or spend your nights searching for answers on the web. You can try a new diet, watch another video, turn your back in anger, or shake your tiny fists at the sky. Or, you can do a much more powerful thing—you can stop doing, close your eyes, let the tears fall, and pray.

37

STANDING ALONE

At my first defense no one stood with me, but all
forsook me. May it not be charged against them.

2 Timothy 4:16

READING: 2 TIMOTHY 4:9-18

The narrow road is such not because it is lacking in space but rather
in companionship. Beginning at salvation and continuing throughout
this life, we are confronted with choices that often result in separation to or from other things and, sadly, other people. A decision to
follow Jesus is the first degree of separation, but the road of discipleship brings many more. There are times throughout this kingdom
life that we end up in spaces where we feel alone: Isolated in our
jobs or ministries. Alone in our problems. Solo in our relationships or
deserted in our fears.

On more than one occasion over the years, my husband and I
have felt led to pack up our few things, corral our young children, and
move across the country from the familiar to the unknown. When we
first arrive in a new place, there is an excitement and thrill that fuels

us through the first weeks of unpacking, shopping, and arranging of new services and things. There are many calls from family and friends that, through the move, were left behind. There are many posts of videos and pictures to share the details of the new place and life. But far too soon, the calls drop off and the exciting chaos settles down into a quiet normalcy. That's when an icy terror creeps into our hearts and minds, and we silently scream, *What did I do?! What was I thinking?! Why am I in Portland without my friends or my mom or my stuff?!* And the ache of loneliness begins to set in.

Paul, in all his giftedness and strength, was also human. He struggled with the loss of comrades and brothers while feeling compelled to go on. Still, he was not ashamed or too proud to reach out or to ask for simple items of comfort to make the journey more bearable.

> "Do your diligence to come shortly to me. . . . The cloak that I left . . . when you come, bring with you, and the books, but especially the parchments."
>
> 2 TIMOTHY 4:9, 13 (DT)

In the midst of it all, there were friends who left. Facing the daily challenges and offenses, poverty and suffering, many people got tired and walked away. Others, like Alexander, added the pain of betrayal.

> At my first defense no one stood with me, but all forsook me.
>
> 2 TIMOTHY 4:16

At one point, Paul was completely alone, as we will sometimes be or feel. Yet, as Paul implies, we must not allow ourselves to slip into self-pity, bitterness, or unbelief. These are the days (or months or years) when our narrow road winds through the wilderness—an often barren, dry, and desolate place. Despite every instinct to the contrary, we should not seek to avoid it. For it is at these times that we are often more clearly aware of God's presence and strength, the truth of his Word, and the depth of the call. And sometimes we experience miraculous deliverance.

The lie of the enemy is that we've been abandoned by God, forgotten and cut off in a cruel and friendless place. We may feel lost in the loneliness of our newly gentrified neighborhood or as the solitary leader of color in the "multicultural" church we attend. We may feel isolated in our poverty or singleness or poor health, or secluded as the only woman director on a board or team of older men. But we are not forsaken, and we will not be destroyed.

While it is unlikely that we can avoid some periods of being alone, that does not mean that we must endure the crippling sorrow of loneliness. Like Paul, we remember the truth that the Lord is with us, and from that we gain strength. We can ask the Father to deliver us from the lion of loneliness to the mysterious peacefulness of solitude. And he will.

There will be points throughout this fight for right and righteousness when we may be abandoned by the fellowship we crave. Yet Immanuel stands near. If we keep moving forward, our path will eventually intersect with like-minded sisters and brothers again—if not here, then on the other side.

38

THE CALL

And He came and preached peace to you who were
afar off and to those who were near. For through Him
we both have access by one Spirit to the Father.

Ephesians 2:17-18

READING: EPHESIANS 2:11-19

It was still dark when I dropped him off outside the Delta entrance of the Portland airport early on a Wednesday morning. In the past decade of our married life, airport runs have become routine—a quick stop, a light kiss, and a promise of a later call from the next destination. And usually on the ride home, I'm moving ahead, thinking about my upcoming errands or the ever-running to-do list in my head. But as much as we tried to treat it the same, everything was different on this morning.

This morning, my glasses fogged as I tried in vain to fight back the tears that were threatening. This morning, my heart ached with the weight of it all. This morning, I could hear my breath in the dark silence of the car, short and rapid with the fear I was trying to push down.

I hated the reason for this trip, the need of it. In my mind were the images of the previous night's news: The words of the obviously frightened reporter, anxiously looking over her shoulder. The angry faces of the crowd, the threatening police decked out in their military garb, the frantic press shuffling from place to place on the hunt for the story. I wanted to say no, don't go. It's not safe. But instead I kissed him goodbye and drove away because despite the possible danger, there was the need. There were the cries from the street. There was the threat of the overwhelming darkness. And there was the call.

> For he himself is our peace, who has made the two groups one and has destroyed the barrier, the dividing wall of hostility. . . . His purpose was to create in himself one new humanity out of the two, thus making peace, and in one body to reconcile both of them to God through the cross, by which he put to death their hostility.
>
> EPHESIANS 2:14-16 (NIV)

Just over a year before, I sat on the edge of my bed in Atlanta, hot tears streaming down my face. The George Zimmerman not-guilty verdict had just been announced, and my children and I, including my black boys—my young adult sons—had watched it together. The shock and horror of it rendered us all speechless. I retreated to my bedroom, wrestling with the awful truth that was becoming all too clear. In my country, my children—all born and raised on American soil, educated in American schools where they saluted American flags, worked at honest jobs where they paid American taxes, regis- tered and voted in their assigned county at American polling places—

had been declared to be of less value than the children of the majority culture, or perhaps of no value at all. Our laws would not protect them. Our government would not protect them. We were, it appeared, on our own.

Still, the family of Trayvon Martin was gracious. There was no violence in the street, just a collective sigh and ache in the soul of our communities. We wiped our tears, swallowed our sorrow, and kept moving.

Unfortunately, forgiveness and grace did not bring repentance because the bodies of our children have continued to fall at the border, on the reservation, and in the streets of urban neighborhoods. The powers that be were ordained by God for good for us, but instead many have chosen to destroy. This cannot continue, because the black and brown child has also been brought near and reconciled by the cross. We too have drunk from the well of living water and been invited to abundant life. Any people and any government in any town anywhere that denies this is an unjust people, government, or town at odds with the King and his kingdom. And we who have been called out and sent as ambassadors of that kingdom must respond. It is for this reason that we have been reborn.

So, despite the pit in my stomach and my shallow breath, I left my love at that airport in the predawn hours as he headed to join the gathering saints in Ferguson, Missouri, for a powerful stance of peaceful resistance. I drove back down the interstate toward home because the kingdom of heaven is suffering violence. Because I have sons and daughters in this America. Because of the call.

39

PLACE OF REFUGE

Your way, O God, *is* in the sanctuary;
Who *is* so great a God as *our* God?

Psalm 77:13

READING: PSALM 77:1-15

Recent years have been hard. Our screens and minds are overwhelmed with the images of police shootings, school shootings, and mass shootings; fires, floods, and hurricanes; crying children and distraught mothers; chain link fences and razor wires. So much pain.

In grief, we cry out to God. Like a tidal wave, the emotion begins in the belly and then swells, filling the chest and then the throat, the mouth, the air. In trouble and despair, confusion or frustration, when God seems far away, we cry out.

Although the temples, chapels, and cathedrals of the world have provided sanctuary for the people of God throughout time, the place of refuge or safety we seek is not a space created below ceilings or between walls. It does not require stained glass or pews, big screens, projectors, or coffee bars. No, we find sanctuary any time when, in the Spirit, we enter the presence of the living God. Sanctuary is the place where we empty our hearts before the Lord, pouring out our pain, anger, and sorrow like water. But it is also a place of remembrance and restoration where we can find and enter that space through worship.

Worship is not a form of entertainment for a crowd of religious spectators. It is the way we remind our souls of who God is and what he has done.

> I will remember the works of the LORD;
> Surely I will remember Your wonders of old.
> I will also meditate on all Your work,
> And talk of Your deeds.
>
> PSALM 77:11-12

The sanctuary is a sacred and holy place where instinctively our heads, knees, and hearts bow in reverence around the altar. The altar provides a table for both communion and sacrifice. There, we remember and consume the broken body and spilled blood of Jesus. There, we offer up our own for healing and divine use. There, we surrender our fears, cares, and worries. There, we recall that we have been given new life. In times like these, we need both physical and figurative altars and sanctuaries within our homes, ourselves, and our communities: places where we can pause to worship, pray, and cry before the living God; places of stillness and quiet; places of beauty and holiness.

Once, my husband and a friend created a prayer labyrinth in the parking lot of a church in an urban Portland neighborhood. The friend, an engineer, laid out the design with stones, and we framed it out with cinder blocks, wooden rails, potted plants, and flowers. Seats and posts were placed in the four corners, encouraging visitors to sit and pray. We prayed for the children of our community, for the police and political leaders of our city, and for the poor and the oppressed throughout the land. As we walked the path of that labyrinth praying, from the start to the center and out again, tears became sighs. Sighs became silence. Silence became peace, and peace became hope.

In the sanctuary, we can *re*-member God. The image and reality of the King of Glory can be reconstructed from the severed pieces. The dismemberment of his identity in our minds and hearts by the trials and circumstances of our lives can be undone, and our faith rebuilt. The sanctuary reminds us of who he is and what he has done, and this reconstructs our hope.

So while I cry out like Asaph at the hardness of the world and perhaps this life, I will return to the sanctuary again and again to remind myself that the Word of God is still true. Jesus is still risen. Our God is yet so great a god. Therefore, will I hope.

40

THE GARDEN OF GRIEF

The spirit indeed *is* willing, but the flesh *is* weak.

Matthew 26:41

READING: MATTHEW 26:36

For a while we had been sensing the restlessness, a familiar warning that God was about to make a significant change in our lives. Still, when my husband shared that the possible next assignment in our kingdom journey would involve moving more than 2,600 miles from our home and church and community and moving our children, I was in shock. How could God do this? We had spent the last fifteen-plus years building a family, ministry, and life in Atlanta. We started literally with next to nothing and had finally reached a place of some stability. Yet here was God again, for the second time, asking us to leave it all and start over somewhere new—somewhere foreign, alone. How do we respond to this? Isn't that a bit much to ask?

> You have not yet struggled to the point of
> shedding blood in your striving against sin.
>
> HEBREWS 12:4 (DT)

In the garden, Jesus was facing a much more devastating assignment. And his response was to gather his posse and head to a quiet place to talk to God. Once there, Jesus, weighed down with grief and despair so much so that he felt like he might die, began to talk to the Father.

> ## This I recall to my mind,
> ## Therefore I have hope.
> ### LAMENTATIONS 3:21

At the thought of Jesus kneeling in the garden, I'm reminded of a time when I was bowed down in grief, facing a God-assignment that felt like too much to bear. The image of me, down on my knees, head in my hands in the pre-dawn hours of the morning is still clear in my mind. I was sobbing into the cushion of a chair in the corner of my Atlanta living room. We had left everything and everyone familiar to start an urban school in the city. It was hard work: twelve-hour days with no pay and little support; a small, resistant faculty; and inadequate resources. I felt disrespected, misunderstood, and insecure. Worst of all, we were far away from the people we loved and the people who loved us. I was trying to be faithful to the call, but I felt I had nothing left to give. At the end of myself, I cried out to God for help.

I was asking for direction. I was longing for a friend. I was looking for financial relief and a change in the people around me. What he gave me instead was what I needed most: an anchor in the midst of my storm.

Most often we are praying for relief, looking for deliverance or a way of escape. However, sometimes God would have us yield the way Jesus yielded to the cross: Until the person is dead to sin but the spirit is alive to God. Until we realize our need. Until we choose to trust in God and his goodness.

The Lord is good to those who wait: Good to the one who seeks him. Good to the one that still hopes and waits without complaint. Good to the one who bears the yoke of suffering, even if rendered speechless by it.

A short time after that dark morning, I traveled to a Christian school conference with our staff. I was so weighed down with my pain that I could barely stand. I got down on the floor in the back of the conference ballroom and prayed. It was a three-day conference, so I told God I would give him my food for the next three days in exchange for a word from him.

From that point forward, in every session or workshop I attended at that conference, God gave me a word of encouragement, manna from on high. Every speaker read a Scripture passage, told a story, or shared a truth that fed me. Despite my lack of physical food, by the middle of the second day I felt revived and renewed—body, soul, and spirit—and ready to return home to complete the work that had been assigned to me.

In the heat of the suffering, it's hard to see clearly. And for some of us it feels as if we are always going through something. In frustration, feeling mistreated or abandoned, we cry out, "Why, God? Why now? Why me? Or why this? Look at all I've done. Look at all I've sacrificed. Where is my blessing? What am I supposed to get from all of this?"

But when we are still and quiet our hearts before him, we discover an amazing truth. The Lord is our portion. He is what we get. He is our inheritance. He has given us himself, and that is enough to cause our hearts to say, "Nevertheless, your will be done."

EPILOGUE

All things were made *and* came into existence through Him;
and without Him not even one thing was made that has come
into being. In Him was life [and the power to bestow life],
and the life was the Light of men. The Light shines on in the
darkness, and the darkness did not understand it *or* overpower
it *or* appropriate it *or* absorb it [and is unreceptive to it].

John 1:3-5 (AMP)

READING: ISAIAH 40:25-31

Over the years and the course of my life, I've heard many justice
people, both young and old, talk about experiencing burnout. And
well-meaning friends and family members suggest that *maybe it's
time for you to do something else because this (the neighborhood or
the work or the issue) is just too much, and after all, you have kids
to consider, and what about your health, and God expects us to use
wisdom, and . . . and . . . and . . .*

The problem is not that there is more darkness. The problem is
that there is less light. Darkness is a constant, ever present and

relentless. However light, like fire, can change, grow, and spread only as long as it is fueled.

What causes lights to burn out? Is it because it gets too dark? No, lights were created to function in darkness. We burn out because we forget that we are not light itself but rather light bulbs, conduits through which light passes or shines. Solar-powered lights do not stop working because the darkness increases or the sun becomes deficient. Rather, they stop functioning because either the mechanism for absorbing the energy and generating electricity or the battery that stores and discharges it into the bulbs has stopped working properly.

The spiritual disciplines of prayer, meditation, Scripture reading, and solitude are our solar panels, the means through which we draw life and light from the Son. It is easy, in the midst of the demands of this world, to allow them to be overshadowed or crowded out. We can press forward on the rush of adrenaline for a time, but eventually we will begin to feel the effects of this neglect.

> **He gives power to the weak,**
> **and to *those who have* no might He increases strength.**
>
> **ISAIAH 40:29**

Every now and again we can get caught up in the demand of deadlines and the tyranny of the urgent. We get convinced that there's no time for our devotional practice. We begin skipping the Bible reading and muttering quick, repetitive prayers. Our worship is limited to the weekly, corporate, hour-and-a-half Sunday gathering. Solitude is found only if, as we race to the next meeting, we decide to turn off the radio in the car. The light within us begins to flicker and become dim.

We are not capable of producing our own light or charging our own batteries. Again and again Jesus, the lord of the universe, slipped away—in the morning or the evening, in a garden or to the mountains—to pray or to mourn, to cry and to rest. And then he returned to the multitudes to minister and heal them. So, too, we his disciples must make time and find place to meet with the living God, to bask in the warmth of his Sonlight, and to find bread. And then we must return to the meat of service. For we, like Christ, were created with purpose, to make him known and to glorify God.

Resistance is not only the refusal to comply with something but also the ability not to be adversely affected by it. We are light bearers, sent to shine in the darkness and, if properly fueled, we will not be overpowered by it.

> But we have this treasure in earthen vessels, that the excellence of the power may be of God and not of us. *We are* hard-pressed on every side, yet not crushed; *we are* perplexed, but not in despair; persecuted, but not forsaken; struck down, but not destroyed—always carrying about in the body the dying of the Lord Jesus, that the life of Jesus also may be manifested in our body. (2 Corinthians 4:7-10)

> Then Jesus said to them, . . . "My Father gives you the true bread from heaven. For the bread of God is He who comes down from heaven and gives life to the world."
>
> Then they said to Him, "Lord, give us this bread always." (John 6:32-34)

ACKNOWLEDGMENTS

Special thanks to David Bailey, Chipper Via, and the talented songwriters and vocalists of Urban Doxology for the beautiful musical contribution to this book (available through the QR codes). For worship leading, internships, or booking information, see www.urbandoxology.com/booking.

NOTES

8: THE FRUIT OF SUCCESS

[1]Assata Shakur, *Assata: An Autobiography* (London: Zed Books Ltd., 1987), 52.

18: EXCEPT YOU BECOME AS CHILDREN

[1]This chapter is adapted from Donna Barber, "Day 2, First Week Fast Reflections," January 11, 2014, Word Made Flesh, wordmadeflesh.org/first-week-fast-reflections.

ABOUT THE AUTHOR

Donna Barber is cofounder of The Voices Project, an organization that influences culture through training and promoting leaders of color. She is also the director of Champions Academy, an initiative of the Portland Leadership Foundation that provides culturally responsive leadership development for student athletes. She is the first African American to serve on her local district's school board. Donna lives in Portland, Oregon, with her husband, Leroy, and their children.

THE VOICES
PROJECT

The Voices Project gathers leaders of color who influence culture (the church, education, art, entertainment, politics, and business) for important conversations about the current challenges and triumphs within communities of color and our role as cultural influencers. We train and promote leaders of color to offer voice to culture and society.

TRAINING AND PROMOTING

We provide insight, on how to be effective in leadership within one's respective area of cultural influence in a way that is rooted in history and experience of people of color. Additionally we connect leaders of color to leadership opportunities that are based in their areas of expertise within a domain of cultural influence.

INITIATIVES

- Mentorship or small group training with Voices staff (ongoing)
- Publishing company (ongoing)
- Bi-annual leadership gathering (January and August)
- Voices Conference (May)
- Northwestern college tour (October)
- Monthly newsletter (ongoing)

THE VOICES PROJECT
255 SW Bluff Dr
Bend, OR 97702
http://www.voices-project.org/

 https://twitter.com/jointhevoices

 https://www.facebook.com/JoinTheVoices/

 https://www.instagram.com/jointhevoices/